Adult Learning Basics

William J. Rothwell

Alexandria, Virginia

13 12 11 10 09 08 1 2 3 4 5 6 7 8

ASTD Press is an internationally renowned source of insightful and practical information on workplace learning and performance topics, including training basics, evaluation and return-on-investment, instructional systems development, e-learning, leadership, and career development.

Ordering information: Books published by ASTD Press can be purchased by visiting our website at store.astd.org or by calling 800.628.2783 or 703.683.8100.

Library of Congress Control Number: 2007939265

ISBN-10: 1-56286-533-1
ISBN-13: 978-1-56286-533-7

ASTD Press Editorial Staff:

Director: Cat Russo
Manager, Acquisitions and Author Relations: Mark Morrow
Editorial Manager: Jacqueline Edlund-Braun
Senior Associate Editor: Tora Estep
Editorial Assistant: Gina Del Priore

Copyeditor: Scott Long
Indexer: April Davis
Proofreader: Kris Patenaude
Interior Design and Production: Kathleen Schaner
Cover Design: Katherine Warminsky
Cover Illustration: Leon Zernitsky

Printed by Victor Graphics, Inc., Baltimore, Maryland, www.victorgraphics.com

Contents

About the *Training Basics* Series

ASTD's *Training Basics* series recognizes and, in some ways, celebrates the fast-paced, ever-changing reality of organizations today. Jobs, roles, and expectations change quickly. One day you might be a network administrator or a process line manager, and the next day you might be asked to train 50 employees in basic computer skills or to instruct line workers in quality processes.

Where do you turn for help? The ASTD *Training Basics* series is designed to be your one-stop solution. The series takes a minimalist approach to your learning curve dilemma and presents only the information you need to be successful. Each book in the series guides you through key aspects of training: giving presentations, making the transition to the role of trainer, designing and delivering training, and evaluating training. The books in the series also include some advanced skills such as performance and basic business proficiencies.

The ASTD *Training Basics* series is the perfect tool for training and performance professionals looking for easy-to-understand materials that will prepare non-trainers to take on a training role. In addition, this series is the perfect reference tool for any trainer's bookshelf and a quick way to hone your existing skills.

Preface

All people learn in pretty much the same way, right? Wrong! Research, theory, practice, and philosophy over many years indicate that people may learn in different ways and may even change how they learn. Children tend to be willing to listen to adults give them information that may not have immediate application. But adults have traditionally been regarded as being much less patient and much more prone to focus on immediate application. They want to know *why* new information is worth knowing and *how to use it.*

Since many trainers and other learning professionals are promoted internally within their organizations, they may lack a solid grounding in adult learning theory, practice, and principles. That can cause problems. There is more to training others than simply throwing grab bags of facts at them. Good trainers should possess an excellent grasp of how to train adults, how training adults is different from training children, and how training older adults may differ from training younger adults.

But what is an adult, and what is an adult learner? Who should read this book? This preface answers these questions, provides chapter-by-chapter highlights to indicate what issues are treated in which chapters, provides an overview of visual icons that are used throughout the book to emphasize key points, and acknowledges the contributions of others who have contributed to this book.

What Is an Adult, and What Is an Adult Learner?

Any book about adult learning should start off with some kind of answers to the questions "What is an adult?" and "What is an adult learner?"

The term *adult* usually means someone who has reached maturity. Of course, there can be a difference between being mature and being of legal age. We sometimes hear people say, "Act your age" to admonish someone to act more mature. Legal age varies by culture and even by location. The key issue in legal age is the age at which an individual may enter into a contract. That is not the same everywhere in the world—or even in every state in the United States.

An *adult learner*, on the other hand, usually implies someone who engages in learning beyond the traditional age of school attendance. Of course, even what is regarded as "traditional school age" can vary. It has been getting older as the U.S. population ages and there are fewer "traditional school-age people" (from ages 7 to 17 for high school and ages 17 to 21 for college). "Average school age" has been on the increase in the United States as people find that a plethora of college graduates leads to a need for higher educational levels to be competitive in the entry-level job market.

But there are several important fallacies to address right at the outset of any book on adult learning. First, while adults may share some things in common, it is a mistake to generalize that all adult learners are the same. They are not. Second, while it is popular to point out generational differences in working and learning styles, the reality is that too little empirical research has been done to indicate differences among so-called Gen X, Gen Y, Gen Z, and all the other various age groups in today's labor market. Care must be taken in making sweeping generalizations about people, since the research to support it is not strong enough to do so with certainty. Third, as the U.S. and global working populations age, interest will increasingly shift from a focus on differences between teaching children and adults to differences among teaching children, adults, and older adults. An *older adult* is an individual beyond traditional retirement age. Some authorities even distinguish among the "young old" (65–75), the "old" (76–85), and the "old old" (86 and up).

Who Should Read This Book?

This book is written for anyone who has occasion to teach, train, coach, or mentor adults or to facilitate groups of adults working together. The audience for this group thus may include

- subject matter experts
- managers
- learning professionals
- HR professionals.

It is important to emphasize that the vast majority of learning occurs on the job. Hence, supervisors, managers, or executives have important roles to play in developing their staff on the job. Being aware of adult learning theory and practice can improve efforts to manage and develop staff members in real time while, at the same time, getting the daily work accomplished.

Chapter-by-Chapter Highlights

Each chapter in this book is intended to contribute to your success as a learning professional who trains, educates, develops, and facilitates adult learning. Here is a summary of the nine chapters:

Chapter 1—"Understanding and Applying Adult Learning Theory" emphasizes the importance of this book and why you should care about it.

Chapter 2—"Using Theory to Design More Effective Training" attempts to answer an age-old question, summarizing what is known about learning theory.

Chapter 3—"Leveraging Adult Learner Differences" summarizes unique issues in learning theory as they apply to adults in workplace settings.

Chapter 4—"Engaging Boomer, Gen X, and Gen Y Learners" seeks to avoid the mistake of generalizing about all adult learning theory. But it does examine some unique differences that may result in learning style and the emergence of different categories of learners.

Chapter 5—"Managing Cultural Differences in Learners" examines cultural issues as they affect adult learners.

Chapter 6—"Making Learning Environment a Key to Success" examines how the learning climate, including the support or lack of support adult learners receive, affects their learning experience.

Chapter 7—"Putting Technology to Work for Learners" describes how instructional technology can affect adult learning. The chapter reviews the so-called *digital divide.*

Chapter 8—"Using Proven Facilitation Techniques to Drive Learning" offers suggestions on facilitating adult learning in various settings—on site, online, and in other formats.

Chapter 9—"Reading the Future of Adult Learning: Seven Hopeful Predictions" invites the reader to consider various trends that may affect future adult learners.

Look for These Icons

This book strives to make it easy for you to understand and apply its lessons. Icons throughout this book help you identify key points.

What's Inside This Chapter

Each chapter opens with a summary of the topics addressed in the chapter. You can use this reference to find the areas that interest you most.

Think About This

These are helpful tips for how to use the tools and techniques presented in the chapter.

Basic Rules

These rules cut to the chase. They represent important concepts and assumptions that form the foundation of adult learning.

Noted

This icon calls out additional information.

Getting It Done

The final section of each chapter supports your ability to take the content of that chapter and apply it to your situation. Sometimes this section contains a list of questions for you to ponder. Sometimes it is a self-assessment tool. And sometimes it is a list of action steps you can take to enhance your facilitation.

Acknowledgments

I dedicate this book to my wife, Marcelina Rothwell, and to my daughter, Candice Rothwell. They light up my life.

I would like to thank Mark Morrow of ASTD for his patience and his encouragement to do this book. I would also like to thank Scott Long for his able help as editor.

Finally, I would like to thank my graduate research assistant, Lin Gao, for her help in securing the necessary copyright permissions for this book.

William J. Rothwell
November 2008

1

Understanding and Applying Adult Learning Theory

What's Inside This Chapter

In this chapter, you'll learn:

- How this book can help you to improve your success in teaching, training, developing, and coaching adult learners
- Why knowing how adults learn is important
- How *training* and *learning* differ
- How learning can affect organizational and individual success.

Most people who work as learning professionals are transferred into it or are promoted into their jobs. They do not possess formal degrees in employee training, human resource development, human performance improvement, or workplace learning and performance (WLP). Most are still not certified professionals in learning and performance. And yet awareness of learning—and how to make it better—is fundamental, and essential, to the work of people in the WLP field. By analogy, medicine is based on a fundamental understanding of human anatomy, and WLP is based on a fundamental understanding of human learning. For learning professionals, learning is a critically important means to the end of improving performance.

The same principle applies to managers. Learning is embedded in everything workers do to achieve results on their jobs. While it may not be acknowledged as such, learning has to do with investigating problems, finding solutions, serving customers, and performing work on a daily basis. Managers have a critically important role to play in staff development, and learning is an important factor in cultivating talented workers for the future.

This book is intended to be a practical primer on adult learning. It is meant to help trainers and learning professionals improve how effectively they do their jobs in using learning to achieve results (performance). It can also provide managers with useful information on what they should know about adult learning. Learning is really at the heart of what people in the WLP field do. It is also at the heart of what most managers must know how to do today if they are to get results from their people, grow talent for the future, and facilitate innovation that leads to competitive advantage.

Why Knowing How Adults Learn Is Important

Most of who we are as human beings is learned; most of what we can do as human beings is also learned. Not surprisingly, then, most of what we do in the world of work has something to do with learning. While some people continue to see a sharp divide between the world of formal schooling and the world of work, lifelong education and lifelong learning have become a reality. As a result of the World Wide Web, all human knowledge now turns over about once every five years—and the *half-life of knowledge* is falling. A day will come in our lifetimes when all human knowledge will turn over several times while an individual progresses through elementary school, middle school, high school, college, and graduate school. In fact, some authorities would argue that day has already arrived when all engineering knowledge turns over even as a typical student progresses through an engineering degree; all medical knowledge turns over during the years that a physician undergoes schooling and practical training; and all legal knowledge turns over even as a lawyer-in-training pursues a juris doctorate and passes the bar exam.

To discover opportunities and solve problems in today's fast-paced, dynamic, knowledge-based business world where everything can change suddenly, workers must use their heads and not (as in the agricultural or industrial age) their hands.

The information age means that workers are devoting most of their time to acquiring, analyzing, and using information in their daily work. That means they must learn to solve practical work-related problems, often in real time.

But how much formal schooling or training has the average manager (or worker) had about learning? Typically, the answer is "very little to none." Teaching principles of adult learning is not embedded in business school curricula or emphasized in business school classes. And yet knowing how to coach, mentor, and direct people to achieve results is central to what managers (and workers) do. Finding, developing, and retaining talent is foundational to an organization's competitive success. And meeting these challenges means that the typical manager must know about adult learning. Learning is also foundational to the success of a worker. But most people have not been given instruction on effective ways to learn.

Think About This

How could people be trained to learn? Organizations have made efforts to improve the quality of on-the-job learning (OJL). Is it possible to train people to learn how to learn better? It may be. Think about adding a module to your organization's onboarding program to encourage people to take initiative to learn—and give them practice in taking the initiative to do that.

How Training and Learning Differ

Training is something done to others. It "pushes" knowledge, skills, and attitudes that are essential to successful work performance. Training changes individuals so that they can get better work results as quickly as possible. It is a short-term, individually oriented change strategy intended to improve a worker's job performance.

But *learning* is something that individuals do on their own. It is a "pull" strategy. Learners "pull" knowledge, skills, and attitudes from others so that they can be successful.

In fact, learning may be as natural for human beings as breathing. Research by Allen Tough (1971) revealed that the typical adult undertakes learning projects to solve real-time work or life problems. Tough concluded that "almost everyone undertakes at least one or two major learning efforts a year, and some individuals undertake as many as 15 to 20. The median is eight learning projects a year, involving eight distinct areas of knowledge and skill" (p. 1). Learners devote from eight to 16 hours on each project. Some people exceeded 2,000 hours in the amount of time they devoted to learning during a six-month period. Tough discovered that learning projects are usually undertaken to master a specific knowledge or skill in anticipation of a work or life need. Most learning projects were directly related to the learners' occupations. Tough found that, in about 75 percent of learning projects, learners assumed most or all responsibility for planning the learning. But these projects are so natural that most people do not even think of them as learning projects, but rather as just part of everyday life.

Basic Rule 1

Training should not be confused with learning. While training is a means to the end of learning, they are simply not the same thing.

A simple example may serve to emphasize this point. Suppose an individual wants to save money. Gas prices increase, and the person seeks a less expensive way to get to work than by driving a car. That is a real-life problem—and one that many people can relate to at a time when gas prices are skyrocketing. To solve the problem, the individual ponders this question: What are some less expensive ways to get to work? The person may then search for information to solve the problem. She may ask her co-workers how they are solving this problem. She may consult the web for ideas to solve the problem. She may look into public transport, trying to find out how easily accessible it is and how much its cost might compare to the cost of a daily drive to work. This simple example is meant to illustrate how learning and problem solving go together. It is thus an example of what Tough would call a learning project. Note that the person must be motivated to learn and must see a reason for doing so.

The same thing happens on the job—sometimes many times daily. A customer calls in with a question. The worker taking the call does not know the answer. To help the customer, the worker tries to find the answer to the question and relay it back to the customer. By doing so, the worker is also learning how to field that question from future customers and may even discover that the organization has not done a good job in addressing the issue that the customer is asking about. That is also a learning project.

How Learning Can Impact Organizational and Individual Success

If learning is about mastering useful knowledge, skills, and attitudes to achieve results, then it is central to organizational and individual success. Neither organizations nor individuals can adapt to change—or take advantage of future opportunities—if they lack the requisite knowledge, skills, and attitudes. As a result, learning is a very important means to the end of performing.

In recent years, much attention has been focused on demonstrating the impact or the return-on-investments in training. But less attention has been focused on demonstrating the impact or return-on-investments in learning. One reason may be that measuring the value of learning may be even more daunting than measuring the value of training. Participation in training can be identified. It is easy to count how many people are sitting in training seats or are logged into online training. And if the training is planned, it is easy to see what people have been taught to do by consulting the measurable instructional objectives. However, it remains to be seen whether they apply what they have been taught back on the job and what measurable value the organization gains when they do that.

But learning is not always as obvious. Much learning is informal. The fruits of organizational learning are embedded in taken-for-granted aspects of corporate culture. *Culture* has to do with the unspoken assumptions about the right and wrong ways to do things. Where did those assumptions come from? The answer is usually "from experience," and that experience is registered in the memories of individuals and in the relics of organizational life (such as policies and procedures). Experience is valued because it is the result of learning. While the value of learning from experience seems obvious, it is more difficult to measure. Whose experience is important? How is experience applied? What do people do with it, and how do they creatively apply what has been learned from experience to new situations?

While measurement difficulties may be apparent in noting the impact of learning on performance, it is clear that individuals—and organizations—usually become more efficient and effective as they gain experience. It is the learning that stems from experience that makes them more efficient and effective. There seems to be little doubt that learning can and does have an impact on organizational and individual performance.

Getting It Done

Chapter 1 emphasized the importance of learning on performance and how learning is embedded in the work experience. Here are some questions to help you develop a mindset for the application of the principles you will learn in the succeeding chapters.

Consider how learning influences your daily work. Can you list some ways this influence is manifested?

1. ______________________________

   ____

2. ______________________________

   ____

How might you measure learning's impact on your own performance?

1. ______________________________

   ____

2. ______________________________

   ____

How might your learning affect the performance of your organization?

1. ______________________________

   ____

2. ______________________________

   ____

2

Using Theory to Design More Effective Training

What's Inside This Chapter

In this chapter, you'll learn:

- How *learning* is defined
- What some different types of learning are
- What theories of learning exist
- How a trainer's philosophy influences practice
- How theories of learning may affect instruction and training
- What model can guide an understanding of the learning process
- What is unique about the mental, physical, and emotional characteristics of adults.

How Is *Learning* Defined?

According to the online edition of the *American Heritage Dictionary* (http://www.ask.com/reference/dictionary/ahdict/64358/learning), *learning* has three main definitions. First, it can mean "the act, process, or experience of gaining knowledge or skill." Second, it can mean "knowledge or skill gained through schooling or study." Third, it can mean "behavioral modification, especially [acquired] through experience or conditioning." *Knowledge* is generally understood to mean facts, information, and concepts. *Skill* refers to know-how—that is, practical awareness of how to do something. *Attitude* is a general disposition or feeling, positive or negative, about something and is closely aligned to opinions and beliefs. Much training is geared to changing what people know (knowledge), what they can do (skills), and what they feel or how they feel (attitudes).

Wikipedia (http://en.wikipedia.org/wiki/Learning) defines learning in a more robust way than the dictionary definition in the previous paragraph. It is "the acquisition and development of memories and behaviors, including skills, knowledge, understanding, values, and wisdom. It is the product of experience and the goal of education. Learning ranges from simple forms of learning such as habituation and classical conditioning seen in many animal species, to more complex activities, such as play, seen only in relatively intelligent animals."

Do these definitions seem inadequate to capture the nuances of a complicated human process? If so, then consider that others have defined learning differently and that, ultimately, understanding of the learning process remains incomplete. According to Hergenhahn and Olson (1997), "*learning* refers to a change in behavior potentiality, and *performance* refers to the translation of this potentiality into behavior" (p. 5). In short, *learning* gives individuals the potential to get results. But *performance* is the actual realization of that potential.

Think About This

Learning is a means to the end of getting results. What are other ways to get results? Consider changing the work setting, changing rewards, changing job design, and changing the tools and equipment workers are given to do their jobs. Making those changes will also affect results. Though learning is an important factor in getting results, it is not the only factor. Can you think of other factors beyond those listed above that may affect the ability of a worker to get results?

What Types of Learning Exist?

Not all learning is the same. While people may differ in how they categorize types of learning, many learning professionals are familiar with Robert Gagné's (1985) distinctions among categories of learning.

Gagné's Types of Learning. For Gagné, the types of learning are arrayed in a hierarchy of complexity. These categories are important because each type of learning typically requires a different type of instruction. Gagné's five major categories of learning are (1) verbal information, (2) intellectual skills, (3) cognitive strategies, (4) motor skills, and (5) attitudes. Different "conditions" are essential for each type of learning. Gagné's theory also outlines nine instructional events and corresponding cognitive processes:

- Gain attention (*reception*)
- Inform learners of the objective (*expectancy*)
- Stimulate recall of prior learning (*retrieval*)
- Present the stimulus (*selective perception*)
- Provide learning guidance (*semantic encoding*)
- Elicit performance (*responding*)
- Provide feedback (*reinforcement*)
- Assess performance (*retrieval*)
- Enhance retention and transfer (*generalization*).

These "events" establish essential conditions for learning and form the basis for instructional design and selection of instructional media. In a more practical sense, they can provide an excellent foundation for planning instruction of any kind.

Fundamental Categories of Learning Behaviors. Wikipedia (http://en.wikipedia.org/wiki/Learning) contains an excellent overview of different types of learning. It distinguishes among several types, including the following:

- **Habituation** is "an example of non-associative learning in which there is a progressive diminution of behavioral response probability with repetition of a

Basic Rule 2

Not all learning is the same. There are different categories of learning. Facilitating different types of learning may require different types of instruction.

stimulus. It is another form of integration. An animal first responds to a stimulus, but if it is neither rewarding nor harmful the animal reduces subsequent responses. One example of this can be seen in small song birds—if a stuffed owl (or similar predator) is put into the cage, the birds initially react to it as though it were a real predator. Soon the birds react less, showing habituation."

- **Sensitization** is "an example of non-associative learning in which the progressive amplification of a response follows repeated administrations of a stimulus. An everyday example of this mechanism is the repeated tonic stimulation of peripheral nerves that will occur if a person rubs his arm continuously. After awhile, this stimulation will create a warm sensation that will eventually turn painful."
- **Operant conditioning** is "the use of consequences to modify the occurrence and form of behavior. Operant conditioning is distinguished from Pavlovian conditioning in that operant conditioning deals with the modification of voluntary behavior. Discrimination learning is a major form of operant conditioning."
- **Classical conditioning** "involves repeatedly pairing an unconditioned stimulus (which unfailingly evokes a particular response) with another previously neutral stimulus (which does not normally evoke the response). Following conditioning, the response occurs both to the unconditioned stimulus and to the other, unrelated stimulus (now referred to as the 'conditioned stimulus'). The response to the conditioned stimulus is termed a *conditioned response.*"
- **Observational learning** recognizes that "the most basic learning process is imitation; one's personal repetition of an observed process, such as a smile. Thus an imitation will take one's time (attention to the details), space (a location for learning), skills (or practice), and other resources (for example, a protected area). Through copying, most infants learn how to hunt (that is, direct one's attention), feed, and perform most basic tasks necessary for survival."

Formal, Informal, and Incidental Learning. It is also worthwhile to distinguish among formal, informal, and incidental learning.

- **Formal learning** occurs in a planned event or series of events. Taking classes toward a degree is a well-known approach to formal learning.
- **Informal learning** occurs through interacting with others, observation, firsthand experience, and other so-called "hands-on" events. These activities

may not be planned, but they are important nevertheless and still represent learning.

- **Incidental learning** occurs as a serendipitous byproduct of experience. If someone is sent to France to learn to speak French, he or she may successfully learn the language. But, at the same time, the experience of traveling there will lead to many other worthwhile experiences, prompting much informal learning. This "accidental" learning is incidental learning.

Taxonomies or Domains of Learning. Another way to think about types of learning is based on *taxonomies*. Most learning professionals have some awareness of instructional objectives, which are set forth at the outset of training to declare what learners should be able to do upon completion of the learning experience. Early efforts to develop instructional objectives—which were called "educational goals"—were organized around different hierarchical levels (types) of learning. Three hierarchies of learning were envisioned. The first, and best known, was focused around *cognitive learning*, having to do with knowing. It consisted of six types of learning: knowledge, comprehension, application, analysis, synthesis, and evaluation (Anderson & Krathwohl, 2001; Bloom & Krathwhol, 1956; Gronlund, 1970). The *affective domain*, relating to feelings, consisted of such levels as attitudes of awareness, interest, attention, concern, responsibility, ability to listen and respond in interactions with others, and ability to demonstrate those attitudinal characteristics or values that are appropriate to the test situation and the field of study. Harrow (1972) proposed six levels of the *psychomotor domain*, having to do with skills. They included reflex, fundamental movements, perceptual abilities, physical abilities, skilled movements, and nondiscursive communication. These taxonomies or domains of learning are another way to understand types of learning. They were an early attempt to classify the behaviors associated with the learning process and are still quite important to the work of most trainers.

Additional interest in types of learning have stemmed from *neuroscience*—sometimes called *learning science*—and what the results of recent research on brain physiology and chemistry reveal that are practical for their implications for learning.

Theories of Learning

Say the word *theory* and most learning professionals will instantly tune out because they think theory is not practical. However, Kurt Lewin, a founder of modern organization development, is often credited for saying that "nothing is so practical as a good theory." What he meant is that theory can guide practice. Therefore, a good theory can guide good practice. It is thus eminently practical.

That point is especially true when thinking about learning theory. How trainers conduct training and how learning professionals carry out other learning and performance change efforts stem from their own theories and philosophies of the learning process, the learners, the learning environment, and the results desired. In short, what we do is guided by theory—whether we choose to admit it or not.

Many books on learning theory have been published over the years. They are foundational courses in achieving teaching certificates, since it is usually assumed that awareness of learning theory can and should guide teaching practice. The same argument can be made for training and other planned learning experiences. Learning professionals should have some awareness of what these theories are, what they mean, and how they may affect practice.

While various approaches exist to categorize theories of learning, a simple one is perhaps to be preferred (Hergenhahn & Olson, 1997):

- Functionalistic theories of learning
- Associationistic theories of learning
- Cognitive theories of learning
- Constructivist theories of learning
- Neurophysiological theories of learning
- Other theories of learning.

No theory is "right" or "wrong." Each has advantages and disadvantages; each implies different roles for learners and facilitators of learning.

Functionalistic Theories of Learning. Functionalists see learning as a way that biological organisms can adapt to their environments. Chief functionalists include

Think About This

Different theories of learning have been proposed. What assumptions does each learning theory make about people, about the learning process, and about how to get work results? Consider these issues while reading about the theories of learning.

Edward Lee Thorndike and B.F. Skinner. While their contributions are numerous, this section will focus only on their major ideas.

Thorndike believed that trial-and-error learning was the most basic form of learning. He reached his conclusion about trial-and-error learning through experiments with animals that were placed in a box and had to provide certain responses to escape it. Animals learned how to escape confinement through many efforts, some happening by accident. Most controversial was Thorndike's contention that ideas do not need to mediate learning and that all mammals, including humans, learn in the same ways.

Thorndike proposed a series of "laws" to explain learning. The *law of readiness* states that entities (animals or humans) will find it satisfying to act when ready to do so, that not acting will be irritating when entities are ready to do so, and entities that are forced to act when unwilling will be irritated. The *law of exercise* states that practice will strengthen connections, and lack of practice will weaken connections. (Thorndike later rejected the law of exercise all together.) The *law of effect* states that rewards will increase relationships or connections/learning, while punishments will decrease relationships or connections/learning. Thorndike later revised the law of effect to state that rewards will increase connections, but punishments will have no effect in strengthening or weakening connections among stimuli. The likelihood that learners will transfer training, according to Thorndike, increases when the environment where the behavior is to be enacted is similar to that in which the learning occurred.

B.F. Skinner, famous as a psychologist, is perhaps best known for the Skinner box used in his animal experiments. Skinner identified two kinds of behavior: operant behavior, which is initiated by an entity on its own, and respondent behavior, which "responds" to an identifiable stimulus. Reflexes are an example of respondent behavior, while most human actions are operant behaviors.

Basic Rule 3

Many learning professionals are concerned about transfer of training from the instructional setting to the work setting. Thorndike was an early advocate of ensuring that the similarities between the two must be great if learning is to be transferred. If the setting in which training is conducted is quite different from the work setting, learners will have trouble transferring what they learned.

Skinner did not believe that human beings have free will, but are conditioned by their environments to respond in predictable ways. To understand a person's behavior, study his or her background. Controlling behavior is simply a matter of controlling the reinforcements that an individual, such as a learner, receives. Behaviors that are reinforced or rewarded are repeated; behaviors that are ignored are extinguished. Punishment does not extinguish a behavior but merely reduces the likelihood of its occurrence.

Associationistic Theories of Learning. Associationists see the world in the way people associate stimuli. Chief associationists include Ivan Pavlov, Edwin Ray Guthrie, and William Estes.

Pavlov is most famous for his experiments with dogs. He paired the sound of a bell with food for a dog. The dog soon associated the sound of the bell with the food, which was apparent because the dog salivated when hearing the bell, even when the food was not present. That led to the view of *unconditioned stimulus* (US) associated with an *unconditioned response* (UR), a natural behavior from an organism, and a *conditioned stimulus* (CS) leading to a *conditioned response* (CR). In Pavlov's famous experiment, the dog was presented with food (US) and a bell (CS). That led to salivation, a UR. Eventually, the dog associated the bell with the food and salivated when the bell was run (CR). This experiment shows how associations and conditioning can lead to learning.

Edwin Ray Guthrie made several contributions to learning theory. He proposed the *law of contiguity*, which stated that people will tend to repeat the same behaviors that worked for them in previous, similar situations. Guthrie believed that practice improved performance and that practice was essential to learn a complicated skill composed of a large number of behaviors. Guthrie also focused attention on forgetting—what some might call "unlearning"—and discovered that, for one behavior to be replaced by another, a different cue (initiating situation) must replace what prompted the response on previous occasions.

William Estes focused attention around developing a *stimulus sampling theory of learning*. Learning consists of an enormous, even infinite, number of stimuli. Transfer of learning, a major focus of the theory, takes place when there are similarities between the learning situation and other situations. Of course, that idea is quite similar to Thorndike's.

Cognitive Theories of Learning. Cognitivists focus on cognition, the process of knowing. Best known of this group are the Gestalt theorists, Edward Tolman, Albert Bandura, and Donald Norman.

Gestalt is a German word for organization. Gestalt theorists were interested in organizations or patterns as perceived by individuals during the learning process. Sometimes called *phenomenology*, Gestalt is about focusing on holistic relationships rather than isolated stimulus-response relationships. It tends to be more subjective, viewing reality as that which is perceived, rather than some external absolute. (Reality is in the eye of the beholder; no universe exists except as perceived by an individual.) Gestalt theorists tend to focus on how people perceive reality, and how learning is a function of perception. Individuals collect information to solve problems, but the solution comes in a flash of intuitive insight.

Edward Tolman was famous for indicating that people learn the "big picture," which he called a *cognitive map*. He rejected the notion of focusing on single stimulus-response relationships, preferring instead to look at bigger patterns. Tolman was also careful to distinguish between *learning* (the potential to perform) and *performing* (the manifestation of that ability). People do not apply their learning unless they have a reason to do so. *Latent learning* is what people have learned but have chosen not to apply.

Albert Bandura is famous for *observational learning* (sometimes called *social learning*). In a simple sense, it is the view that people learn by watching others and then trying to imitate them. It is the basis for behavioral modeling in training and has important implications for coaching and mentoring. People remember what they have observed in images and in words. Once an individual has watched someone else perform, he or she needs to practice—engage in a *behavior rehearsal*—to "try it out." To learn, people must be willing to observe others, know who and what to watch, care about what they are watching, and be willing to practice the behaviors that are to be imitated. When applying social learning theory, learning professionals must take care to expose learners not only to good examples but also to the most common bad examples of behavior so that learners can see the difference.

Donald Norman is credited with being the most prominent of learning theorists who advocated an information processing view of learning. Like machines or systems, individuals receive input (information), process it (learn), and then take action (apply it).

Constructivist Theories of Learning. Constructivists focus on how learners internalize what they have learned. Jean Piaget is often regarded as a key exponent of this now well-regarded theory of learning. Piaget described the means by which learners internalize knowledge. Learners construct knowledge from *accommodation* and *assimilation*.

According to the theory, accommodation is the process of reframing one's mental representation of the external world to fit new experiences. Accommodation can be understood as the mechanism by which failure leads to learning: when we act on the expectation that the world operates in one way and it violates our expectations, we often fail. But by accommodating this new experience and reframing our model of the way the world works, we learn from the experience of our own or others' failure.

When individuals assimilate, they incorporate the new experience into an already existing framework without changing that framework. This may occur when individuals' experiences are aligned with their internal representations of the world but may also occur as a failure to change a faulty understanding. For example, they may not notice events, may misunderstand input from others, or may decide that an event is a fluke and is therefore unimportant as information about the world. In contrast, when individuals' experiences contradict their internal representations, they may change their perceptions of the experiences to fit their internal representations.

Constructivists tend to focus on the individual learner, seeking information about individual needs and individual backgrounds. Constructivists place importance on the national culture of individuals, conceding that what and how people learn is greatly influenced by the national cultural settings and the contexts in which they learn. Learners should be more responsible for learning than teachers. Learners are motivated to learn only when they believe they can be successful. Instructors should enact the role of facilitators by guiding and stimulating learners, not by acting like subject matter experts who merely present information to learners.

Neurophysiological Theories of Learning. Neurophysiologists focus on brain anatomy and chemistry and on such complex phenomena as intelligence, thinking, and learning. Donald Hebb is sometimes cited as a leading thinker and advocate of these theories. Initially, Hebb focused on how cells in the brain operate during the learning process. He came to believe that learning was of two types. One type was simple associationism—that is, a stimulus and response were paired. But a second type involved more sophisticated, cognitive processes. Hebb believed that childhood and adult learning were not the same. Childhood learning is primarily the first type of learning. But adult learning is more sophisticated. It involves creative thinking, which is not possible when individuals lack previous knowledge or experience.

Hebb also investigated sensory deprivation. He discovered that individuals require input from the external environment. Without it, their identities begin to disintegrate. In one study, for instance, Hebb paid college students to do nothing but lie on a bed with translucent plastic over their eyes and gloves on their hands to minimize sensation. They could take time out only for short periods to eat and visit the restroom. Few of the research subjects could tolerate these conditions for longer than two or three days. If they lasted longer than that, they began to hallucinate.

Other Theories of Learning. Many academics in the workplace learning and performance field have devoted their careers to establishing and testing theories of learning that may be applied to training and other learning efforts. Few of these theories fit neatly into any one category described above. But they are worthwhile for learning professionals to know about, because they may guide thinking about adult learning. (A thorough description of these theories can be found on the web at http://tip.psychology.org/theories.html. Only a few are summarized here.)

Anchored instruction maintains that the best learning occurs when learners are given an anchor (focus) for it. In practical terms, that means they should be given a specific case, role play, activity, exercise, or other problem-solving situation. They will learn best when given this anchor. Learners should be encouraged to explore and give free play to the mind in a learning situation. Exploration is closely akin to play for children. It allows the exercise of creative thinking.

Cognitive load theory offers the notion that learning happens best when aligned with how people think (cognition). People should not be encouraged to memorize. Instead, they should be helped to learn by being given schemas or structures that help them remember. When teaching complicated topics, instructors should be sensitive to the complexity of the material and seek out ways to make it easier to understand. That may include using multiple examples, graphics, or other aids. Experts and novices perform differently because experts have developed schemas by which to understand what they are doing and navigate through complexity rapidly and efficiently.

Conversation theory was developed by Gordon Pask (1975). To Pask, people (and machines) learn through conversation. Perhaps the most well-known aspect of conversation theory is that people learn best when asked to teach what they have learned back to others. This gives proof to the old saying that "the best way to learn is to teach it to someone else."

Experiential learning was founded by Carl Rogers and, along with the work of Malcolm Knowles, has had a tremendous impact on the field of adult learning. Rogers believed that the most important learning is applied, coming from experience. All people have the capacity to learn, and learning is related to the human need to grow and achieve one's potential. Instructors must ensure that learners have a psychologically supportive climate in which to learn, explain why learning is important, serve as a resource agent to organize resources for learners to use in a learning event or project, and ensure there is a balance sustained between learner feelings and knowledge. Learners should have a major say in how the instruction is designed and delivered, and learners are the best judges of how effective the learning experience was.

Tom Sticht's *functional context approach* to learning emphasizes relating what is to be learned and what work the learner does. One technique favored by this approach is to derive instructional material directly from the work materials that learners use on their jobs. For example, teach writing by directly using emails, reports, and other information that learners use; teach public speaking by directly relating speaking principles to the oral reports required for workers in the learner group; and teach arithmetic by drawing directly from the arithmetic problems that workers face on the job (Carnevale, Gainer, & Meltzer, 1990).

John Carroll has proposed *minimalist learning theory*. The basic idea is that learning events should minimize how much time is devoted to starting a learning event. Instead, learners should immediately be confronted with a learning challenge. Learners should be given self-contained learning projects that are akin to those they face in the real world. The notion is to minimize how much instructional material learners are given and emphasize their own problem solving and exploration. However, learners should also be given tips on how to avoid typical mistakes (Carroll, 1998).

Jean Lave introduced *situated learning*, which has had a profound impact on the training world. Learning should be embedded—that is, situated—in the work setting, culture, and situation in which it is to be applied. How people interact during learning is critical to the process (McLellan, 1995).

David Ausubel (1963) has developed *subsumption theory*, which has also had a profound impact on training. It is about how individuals master massive amounts of material in the shortest time possible. New ideas are subsumed under what learners already know. Ausubel is most famous for introducing the idea of *advance organizers* in which learners are given a roadmap by which to navigate through a large amount of material. An example might be a simple outline offered before a course is delivered to show how all the parts of the course relate to other parts—an approach that resembles what Gestalt theorists also advocate.

How Does a Trainer's Philosophy Influence Practice?

After reading about the theories of learning, you should realize that it is important to reach conclusions about your own beliefs. What trainers and adult educators believe about what they can do does influence their behavior. What do *you* believe about the following:

- The goals and purposes of training?
- The role of training in advocating values, beliefs, ethics, and attitudes?
- Which feedback systems should be used with learners, and why some are better than others?
- Learners?
- Trainers?
- The learning process?
- Training methods and approaches?
- The role of the work environment in training transfer?
- Other key issues that affect what trainers do?

How you answer these questions shapes your personal philosophy of training and learning, and that philosophy, in turn, shapes how you approach the work of trainer.

What do *you* believe about the following:

- The importance of learner individuality as it shapes the learning experience?
- The importance of the culture and previous background/experience of the learner as they shape a learning experience?
- Who bears chief responsibilities for learning?
- What the trainer's role is in the learning process?
- What the learner's role is in the learning process?
- What the role of the learner's supervisor is in the learning process?
- What the role of the work group is in supporting the learning process?
- What the role of the organization's leadership is in supporting the learning process?
- What the role of motivation is in the learning process?

- How important the timing of learning experiences is?
- What the primary role of instructor/trainer/facilitator is and should be?
- What the nature of the learning process is?
- How important work context and corporate or national culture is to the learning process?
- How learners should be engaged in learning?
- How learning experiences should be evaluated and by whom?
- What other issues might be considered that may influence your own views of the trainer's role? The learner's role? The organization's role?

Use the worksheet shown in Exhibit 2-1 to record your own answers to these questions and thus begin to articulate your own philosophy of learning.

How Theories of Learning May Affect Instruction and Training

Every theory of learning and every individual philosophy of teaching influences what trainers or learning professionals do on a daily basis. Important practical ideas may be obtained by contemplating various theories of learning. Hence, theories of learning affect the practice of training and the learner's practice of learning.

Think of it this way: Every theory of learning offers some practical ideas about what trainers/facilitators should do and what learners should do. What follows are some tips based on the theories of learning.

Tips for Trainers Based on the Functionalistic Theories of Learning. Trainers should

- work to give learners a reason to learn—show them why
- encourage people to practice what they learned
- find ways to reward learners for what they learn
- don't punish learners who fail.

Tips for Trainers Based on Associationistic Theories of Learning. Trainers should

- use practice to build skill
- use different cues to help people unlearn what they have previously learned when necessary
- take steps to increase transfer of learning by ensuring that the learning environment is as close as possible to the actual conditions of the work setting in which the learning is to be applied.

Exhibit 2-1: What Is Your Philosophy of Learning?

Directions: For each question listed in the left column below, provide your answer in the right column.

	Questions What do *you* believe about the following:	Answers
1	The importance of learner individuality as it shapes the learning experience?	
2	The importance of the culture and previous background/experience of the learner as they shape a learning experience?	
3	Who bears chief responsibilities for learning?	
4	What the trainer's role is in the learning process?	
5	What the learner's role is in the learning process?	
6	What the role of the learner's supervisor is in the learning process?	
7	What the role of the work group is in supporting learning?	
8	What the role of the organization's leadership is in supporting the learning process?	
9	What the role of motivation is in the learning process?	
10	How important the timing of learning experiences is?	
11	What the primary role of the instructor/trainer/facilitator is and should be?	
12	What the nature of the learning process is?	
13	How important work context and corporate or national culture is to the learning process?	
14	How learners should be engaged in learning?	
15	How learning experiences should be evaluated and who should do that?	
16	What other issues might be considered that may influence your own views of the trainer's role? The learner's role? The organization's role?	

Tips for Trainers Based on Cognitive Theories of Learning. Trainers should

- encourage learner intuition
- organize instruction around pictures of the whole (whole-to-part learning)
- provide learners with cognitive maps by taking steps to try to understand how people understand the big picture
- guide learners to watch those who are successful at performing observable tasks to encourage social learning
- use behavioral modeling to encourage social learning
- encourage learners to try out what they are learning by doing behavioral rehearsals.

Tips for Trainers Based on Constructivist Theories of Learning. Trainers should

- get to know learners and try to understand their backgrounds, since where they come from and where they sit in an organization will influence what they want to learn and how they will use what they learn
- familiarize themselves with the national culture in which people learn, since it will influence what they learn, how they learn, and what they expect of learning situations
- encourage learners to reflect on how new ideas can be incorporated into what they already know, thereby encouraging assimilation
- help learners make sense of mistakes or failures so as to learn from them
- help learners take more responsibility for the learning process instead of expecting trainers to guide learning events
- encourage learners by showing them they can learn and achieve success from the learning process
- play the role of facilitators rather than subject matter experts.

Tips for Trainers Based on Neurophysiological Theories of Learning. Trainers should

- become familiar with differences between adult learners and children as learners
- emphasize sensory input, enriching training experiences by trying to appeal to as many senses as possible to increase retention and transfer of training.

Tips for Trainers Based on Other Theories of Learning. Trainers should apply

- anchored instruction by centering learning experiences on a focal problem-solving activity to make the learning event action oriented
- cognitive load theory by studying how people think and then aligning the design of learning events accordingly, avoiding memorization, and relying instead on multiple examples, graphics, or other aids
- conversation theory by encouraging social interaction among learners and giving them chances to teach back what they have learned
- experiential learning by encouraging action-oriented learning, creating a psychologically supportive learning climate, giving learners compelling reasons to learn, serving as resource agents to put learners in touch with helpful resources to use in their own learning projects, and giving learners a major role in determining how instruction will be designed, delivered, and evaluated
- the functional context approach by drawing instructional materials and activities from real-world situations and from real-world documents or problems
- minimalist learning theory by focusing as soon as possible at the outset of learning on action-oriented, problem-solving challenges, reducing reliance on lectures and increasing reliance on having the learners undertake challenges, and providing tips on how to avoid common mistakes or missteps in the learning process
- subsumption theory by giving learners advance organizers so they will have a roadmap by which to navigate through material they are to learn.

Of course, other learning theories can also have implications for trainers. What is important when deciding what theory to use is the nature of the learning challenge. For instance, complex tasks to be learned may draw on minimalist or subsumption theory; verbal tasks may be learned best using situated learning or the functional context approach.

Key points about each theory of learning and tips on applying them are found in Exhibit 2-2.

Exhibit 2-2: A Summary of Theories of Learning and Tips on Applications

Theory of Learning	Key Idea of the Theory	Tips on Applying the Theory ***Trainers should...***
Functionalistic Theories of Learning	Learning is a way that biological organisms adapt to their environments.	• work to give learners a reason to learn—that is, show them why • encourage people to practice what they learned • find ways to reward learners for what they learn • not punish learners who fail.
Associationistic Theories of Learning	The world is seen in the ways people associate stimuli.	• use practice to build skill • use different cues to help people unlearn what they have previously learned • take steps to increase transfer of learning by ensuring that the learning environment is as close as possible to the actual conditions of the work setting in which the learning is to be applied.
Cognitive Theories of Learning	The focus is on cognition, the process of knowing.	• encourage learner intuition • organize instruction around pictures of the whole (whole-to-part learning) • provide learners with cognitive maps by taking steps to try to understand how people understand the big picture • guide learners to watch those who are successful at performing observable tasks to encourage social learning • use behavioral modeling to encourage and shape social learning • encourage learners to try out what they are learning by doing behavioral rehearsals.
Constructivist Theories of Learning	The focus is on how learners internalize what they have learned.	• get to know learners and try to understand their backgrounds, since where they come from and where they sit on the organization chart will influence what they want to learn and how they will use what they learn • familiarize themselves with the national culture in which people learn, since it will influence what they learn, how they learn, and what they expect of learning situations • encourage learners to reflect on how new ideas can be incorporated into what they already know, thereby encouraging assimilation

Theory of Learning	Key Idea of the Theory	Tips on Applying the Theory *Trainers should...*
Constructivist Theories of Learning (continued)	The focus is on how learners internalize what they have learned.	• help learners make sense of mistakes or failures so as to learn from them • help learners take more responsibility for the learning process instead of expecting trainers to guide learning events • encourage learners by showing them they can learn and achieve success from the learning process • play the role of facilitators who pose questions to stimulate learners' thinking rather than subject matter experts who merely provide information through lecture.
Neurophysiological Theories of Learning	The focus is on brain anatomy and chemistry and on such complex phenomena as intelligence, thinking, and learning.	• become familiar with differences between adult learners and children as learners • emphasize sensory input, enriching training experiences by trying to appeal to as many senses as possible so as to increase learner retention and transfer of training.
Anchored Instruction	The best learning occurs when learners are given an anchor (focus) for it. Instruction should be centered on a specific case, role play, activity, experiential exercise, or other problem-solving situation.	• center learning experiences on a focal problem-solving activity to make the learning event action oriented.
Cognitive Load Theory	Learning happens best when aligned with how people think (cognition).	• study how people think and then align the design of learning events accordingly • avoid memorization and rely instead on multiple examples, graphics, or other aids.
Conversation Theory	People learn through conversation.	• encourage social interaction among learners, and give learners chances to teach back what they have learned.

(continued on next page)

Exhibit 2-2: A Summary of Theories of Learning and Tips on Applications (continued)

Theory of Learning	Key Idea of the Theory	Tips on Applying the Theory *Trainers should...*
Experiential Learning Theory	The most important learning comes from experience.	• encourage action-oriented learning • create a psychologically supportive learning climate • give learners compelling reasons to learn • serve as resource agents to put learners in touch with helpful resources to use in their own learning projects • give learners a major role to play in determining how instruction will be designed, delivered, and evaluated.
Functional Context Theory	What is to be learned should relate to what work the learner does.	• draw instructional materials and activities from real-world situations and from real-world documents or problems.
Minimalist Learning Theory	Learning events should minimize how much time is devoted to starting a learning event. Instead, learners should immediately be confronted with a learning challenge.	• focus as soon as possible at the outset of learning on action-oriented, problem-solving challenges • reduce reliance on lectures • increase reliance on having the learners undertake challenges • provide tips on how to avoid common mistakes or missteps in applying what they have learned.
Subsumption Theory	New ideas are subsumed under what learners already know. Learners should be given advance organizers at the outset of instruction—a roadmap by which to navigate through the material.	• give learners advance organizers so they will have a roadmap by which to navigate through the information they are to learn.

A Model of the Learning Process

It is difficult to discuss a concept as difficult to comprehend as learning without some kind of model to help describe it. A model makes a complicated concept easier to understand. Hence, a model of the learning process makes it easier to understand what learning is and how it occurs.

Educational psychologists have devoted much time and attention to researching learning as a classroom-based phenomenon. Since most trainers, workers, and managers share formal schooling as a common frame of reference, it is not surprising that learning—even in work settings—is confused with schooling. Similarly, models of the learning process tend to imply classroom settings.

What is needed is a model that depicts the complexities of learning in real-time work situations that is also broad enough to include learning in planned learning experiences, such as classrooms or online courses. Consider the model appearing in Exhibit 2-3 and described below.

Experiencing a triggering circumstance is the first step of the workplace learning process. The trigger is anything that leads an individual learner to recognize the importance of learning something new. Without a trigger, the individual ignores stimuli. But when it dawns on the worker that he or she is confronting an issue of importance, then the first step is taken in the learning process.

Recognizing the importance of the issue is the second step of the workplace learning process. The individual grows aware of why knowing more about the issue or problem might be useful. It may not be a formal process; rather, the individual simply realizes that pursuing more knowledge or skill may be beneficial to meet future as well as present needs.

Becoming more curious is the third step in the workplace learning process. Individuals simply become driven to find out more. They ask themselves many questions, such as the following:

- Who would care about this issue?
- Why should I care about it?
- What are its parameters? Does it have parts? What are the parts?
- When would it be most beneficial to know more about this issue?
- Where would knowledge or skill about this issue be most useful?
- How would knowledge about the issue be found?

In short, the learner becomes motivated to discover more about the issue or problem.

Exhibit 2-3: The Workplace Learning Process

The Workplace Learning Process

- **Step 1:** Experience a Triggering Circumstance
- **Step 2:** Recognize the Importance of the Issue
- **Step 3:** Become More Curious
- **Step 4:** Seek Information
- **Step 5:** Process Information
- **Step 6:** Convert or Transform Information into Useful Knowledge
- **Step 7:** Apply the Knowledge
- **Step 8:** Remember What Was Learned
- **Step 9:** Reflect on What Was Learned
- **Step 10:** Evaluate the Learning Experience

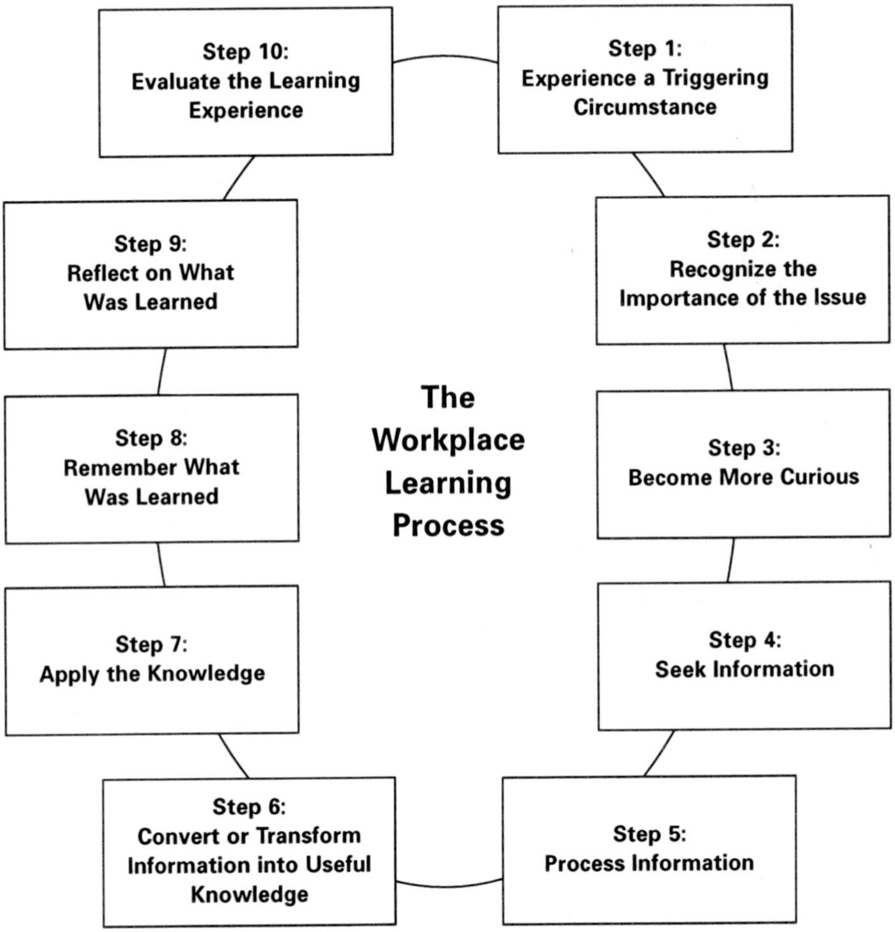

Source: Adapted from Rothwell, W.J. (2002). *The Workplace Learner.* New York: AMACOM.

Seeking information is the fourth step of the process in the workplace learning process. Individuals set out to discover more. They may do that by asking others or by consulting written, electronic, or oral sources of information. Generational differences may exist in that younger people may think first of doing a web-based search, while older people might think of consulting books or print publications.

Processing information is the fifth step of the workplace learning process, and it may coincide with or follow the fourth step. Individuals try to make sense of what they have discovered from their information search about the issue or problem. By organizing and internalizing the information, they begin to understand it better.

Converting or transforming the information into useful knowledge is the sixth step of the workplace learning process. Individuals ask themselves, "What does the information I have found mean? How can it be interpreted and used?"

Applying the knowledge is the seventh step of the workplace learning process. Individuals decide to do something to rehearse using the new information. In short, they experiment with it. That may mean they apply a simple pilot test. Alternatively, they may try to use the information to solve a current or pending problem they face in their lives or on their jobs.

Remembering what was learned is the eighth step of the workplace learning process. Learners store the fruits of their experience for future application. Memory becomes quite important at this stage. There is short-term memory and long-term memory. *Short-term memory* is stored for only a short time. About 80 percent of what people hear or learn is forgotten within 48 hours. *Long-term memory* is stored for future use and is critical in making work experience valuable. The fruits of work experience are made manifest by long-term memory. The collective long-term memory of an organization is reflected in its corporate culture.

Reflecting on what was learned is the ninth step of the workplace learning process. Learners do not always reflect on who was instrumental in the learning process, what they learned, when they learned it, where they learned it, why they learned it, how they learned it, and how valuable the learning experience was. But reflection is critical to the learning process, because thinking about learning is a first step toward improving it and leveraging it.

Evaluating the learning experience is the 10th and final step of the workplace learning process. Just as step nine is not always taken in every learning situation, so many learners do not take the opportunity to evaluate what they learned. If the goal of the learning process was to meet an immediate need, then individuals will seldom reflect on the value of the learning experience. But if the learning was tied to dramatic emotions, then often people will evaluate their own learning experiences.

Applying a Model of the Workplace Learning Process

Many learning professionals will ask, "Why should we care about a model of the workplace learning process?" The answer to that question is worthy of emphasis. If it is clear how people learn, then learning professionals can be more successful in organizing planned learning experiences so that people will be encouraged to move through all the key steps of the learning process. In short, learning professionals should integrate what they do with how learners master new knowledge, skills, or attitudes.

To do that, learning professionals should plan learning experiences based on the learning process model. Hence, the learning professionals' role in planned learning should be to facilitate the steps in the learning process. Consider the model appearing in Exhibit 2-4 and described below.

Step 1: To facilitate experiencing a triggering circumstance, learning professionals should open a planned learning experience with a compelling effort to capture learners' attention.

Step 2: To facilitate recognizing the importance of the issue, learning professionals should emphasize the importance of the issue to the individual learner and to the business, division, department, or team. That means more than glib references to company needs. It is best to appeal to individual self-interest and show how learning something affects an individual.

Step 3: To facilitate a process of piquing learners' curiosity, learning professionals should lead learners to consider questions that will help them understand the full complexity of the issue.

Step 4: To facilitate a process of getting learners to seek information, learning professionals should supply suggestions about how learners could find out more.

Step 5: To facilitate the processing of information, learning professionals should help learners interpret and critically examine information they have found.

Step 6: To facilitate learners' process of converting or transforming the information into useful knowledge, learning professionals can encourage learners to explore the meaning of the information they have found and interpret it.

Step 7: To facilitate how learners apply the knowledge they have acquired, learning professionals can provide structures by which learners can experiment with or try out what they have learned.

Step 8: To assist learners in remembering what they learned, learning professionals can help learners develop memory joggers, job aids, or performance support tools that will enable them to apply what they have learned.

Step 9: To encourage learners to reflect on what they learned, learning professionals can structure situations that will encourage such reflection. This can be done by asking them to reflect on their learning process and consider ways to improve it in the future.

Exhibit 2-4: Applying the Workplace Learning Process

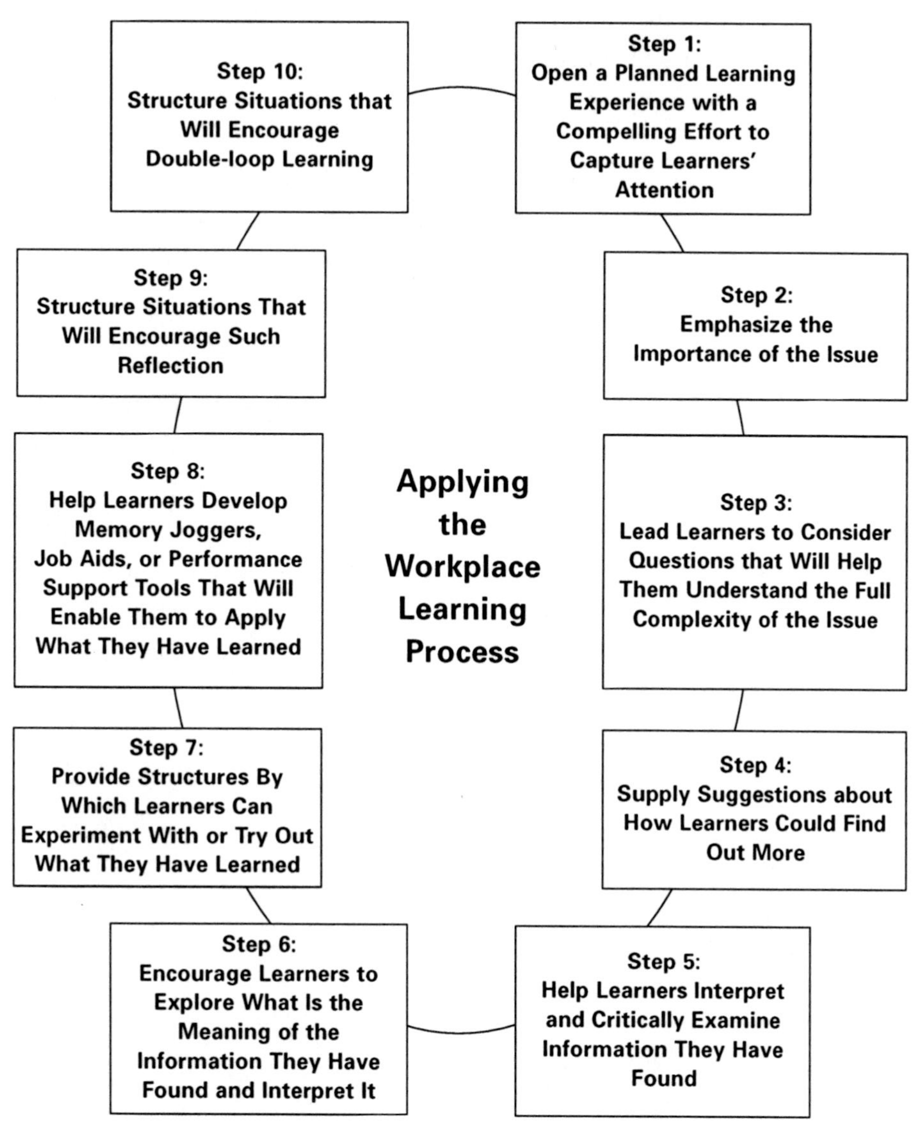

Source: Adapted from Rothwell, W.J. (2002). *The Workplace Learner.* New York: AMACOM.

Step 10: Finally, to help learners evaluate the learning experience and reflect on how they could improve their ability to learn how to learn, learning professionals can structure situations that will encourage double-loop learning.

Use the lesson planning tool appearing in Exhibit 2-5 as a means to apply the model.

The models we have discussed can be integrated. This will encourage individuals to take responsibility for their own learning process and help learning professionals organize planned learning events. Consider the integrated model appearing in Exhibit 2-6.

What Is Unique About the Mental, Physical, and Emotional Characteristics of Adults?

Adults undergo different challenges as they progress through their lives. This view is the foundation for the developmental view of learning. In short, people progress through life cycles. They are thus more motivated to learn about issues that affect the central life challenges of their times of life.

An early statement of this belief was made by William Shakespeare in his play *As You Like It* (act 2, scene 7):

> All the world's a stage,
> And all the men and women merely players:
> They have their exits and their entrances;
> And one man in his time plays many parts,
> His acts being seven ages. At first the infant,
> Mewling and puking in the nurse's arms.
> Then the whining school-boy, with his satchel
> And shining morning face, creeping like snail
> Unwillingly to school. And then the lover,
> Sighing like furnace, with a woeful ballad
> Made to his mistress' eyebrow. Then a soldier,
> Full of strange oaths, and bearded like the pard,
> Jealous in honor, sudden and quick in quarrel,
> Seeking the bubble reputation
> Even in the cannon's mouth. And then the justice,
> In fair round belly with good capon lined,
> With eyes severe and beard of formal cut,

Exhibit 2-5: Lesson Plan Format Based on Applying the Workplace Learning Process

Directions: For each question listed in the left column below, provide your answer in the right column. By doing so, you will use the workplace learning process as a basis for developing a lesson plan.

	Questions	Answers
1	How can you, as facilitator, open a planned learning experience with a compelling effort to capture learners' attention?	
2	How can you, as facilitator, emphasize the importance of the issue?	
3	How can you, as facilitator, lead learners to consider questions that will help them understand the full complexity of the issue?	
4	How can you, as facilitator, supply suggestions about how learners could find out more?	
5	How can you, as facilitator, help learners interpret and critically examine information they have found?	
6	How can you, as facilitator, encourage learners to explore the meaning of the information they have found and interpret it?it	
7	How can you, as facilitator, provide structures by which learners can experiment with or try out what they have learned?	
8	How can you, as facilitator, help learners develop memory joggers, job aids, or performance support tools that will enable them to apply what they have learned?	
9	How can you, as facilitator, structure situations that will encourage reflection?	
10	How can you, as facilitator, structure situations that will encourage double-loop learning?	

Source: Adapted from Rothwell, W.J. (2002). *The Workplace Learner.* New York: AMACOM.

Full of wise saws and modern instances;
And so he plays his part. The sixth age shifts
Into the lean and slipper'd pantaloon,
With spectacles on nose and pouch on side,
His youthful hose, well saved, a world too wide
For his shrunk shank; and his big manly voice,
Turning again toward childish treble, pipes
And whistles in his sound. Last scene of all,
That ends this strange eventful history,
Is second childishness and mere oblivion,
Sans teeth, sans eyes, sans taste, sans every thing.

Similar views of the stages of human life have appeared in such widely diverse books as *Aesop's Fables*, the *Tales of the Brothers Grimm*, and the *Talmud*.

In modern times, the notion of stages of life development has appeared in the works of psychologists Eric Erikson (1994) and Daniel Levinson (1978) and popular writer Gail Sheehey (2006). In 1956, Erikson presented his view of eight stages of development for children and teenagers. He based his theory on his personal counseling experience rather than on empirical research.

Erikson's first stage is learning *basic trust versus basic mistrust (hope)*. This stage occurs during the first one to two years of life. A young child must learn trust in others—or else the child will become insecure and distrustful of others.

The second phase is learning *autonomy versus shame (will)*. This stage falls somewhere between 18 months and 2 to 4 years of age. A child who has good parents will learn how to function with some self-confidence, but not so much as to ignore all parental guidance.

The third phase is learning *initiative versus guilt (purpose)*. This stage occurs just prior to entry into school. Healthy children learn how to exercise imagination, cooperation, and leadership. But children may also find themselves paralyzed by self-doubt and will be fearful, depending too much at times on adults.

The fourth phase is learning *industry versus inferiority (competence)*. Erikson believes that this phase occurs during school age. Children must learn how to relate to their peers, move beyond free-form play activities to mastery of team-based sports, and learn many educational lessons that will provide the foundation for future schooling.

Exhibit 2-6: Integrating the Workplace Learning Process and Applying It

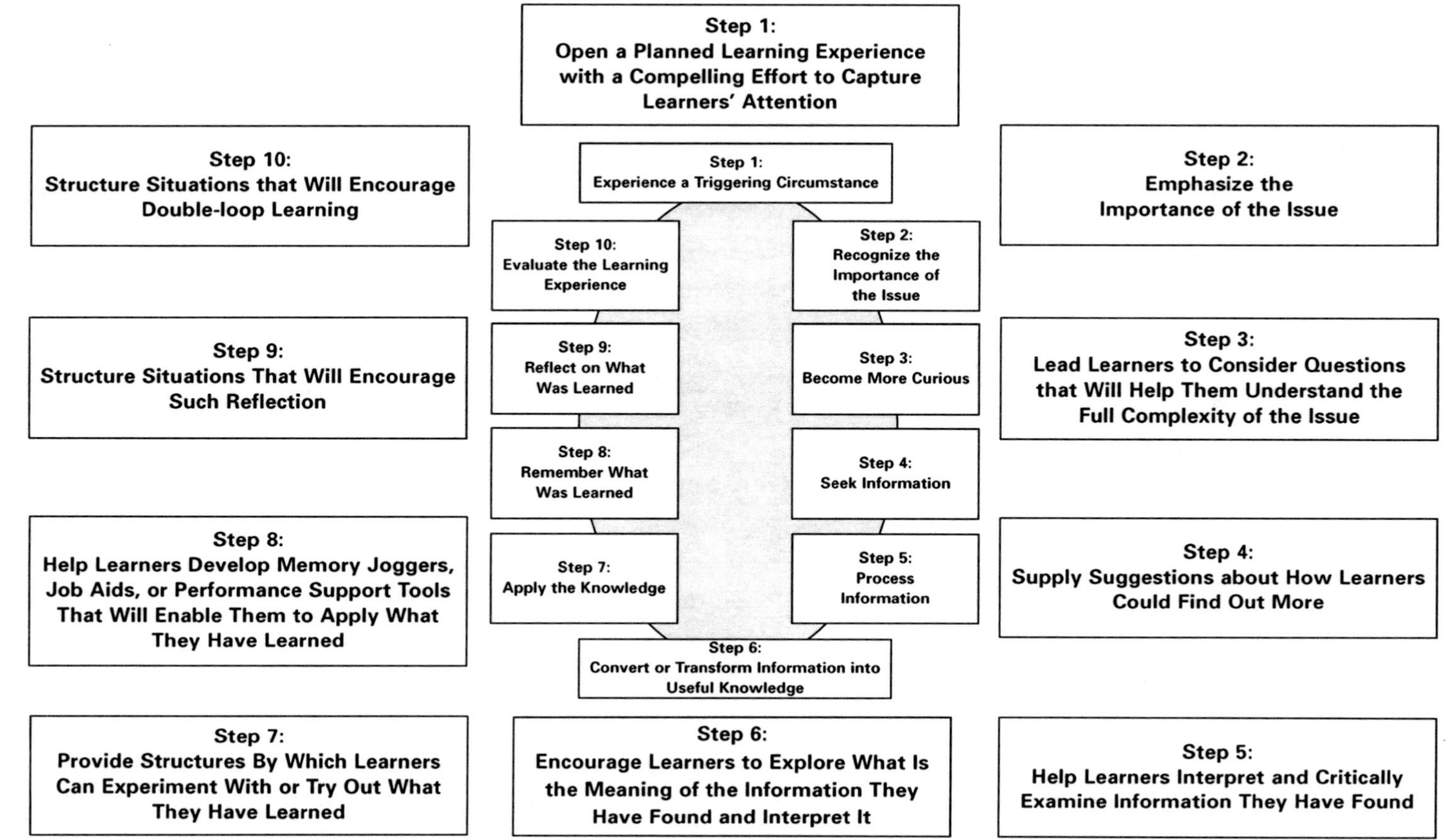

Source: Adapted from Rothwell, W.J. (2002). *The Workplace Learner.* New York: AMACOM.

The fifth phase is learning *identity versus identity diffusion (fidelity).* This phase emerges during adolescence. The adolescent must gain a sense of self-identity, differentiating from peers and parents. But all adolescents face self-doubt and uncertainty about how to cope with the challenges of the future. Gender identity emerges and forms, influenced by societal expectations and norms.

The sixth phase is learning *intimacy versus isolation (love).* To make the transition from adolescent to adult, individuals must discover how to experience intimacy. That intimacy leads to successful (or unsuccessful) marriages and friendships.

The seventh phase is learning *generativity versus self-absorption (care).* Individuals must learn how to function with adaptability in their relationships. If they do not, they will remain self-absorbed.

The eighth and final phase is learning *integrity versus despair (wisdom).* If previous social crises have been resolved, mature adults can be independent, trusting, innovative, and function in groups with a minimum of self-doubt and self-absorption.

These eight stages indicate the central life challenges that emerge at different points in life. The most effective learning experiences will help individuals resolve their conflicts and emerge as people who can be self-directed learners.

The works of Levinson and Sheehey focus primarily on mature adults. Both authors see mature adults as fighting a battle between what they dreamed as children and their own fatal character flaws. There comes a point in life when individuals confront a midlife crisis between the dream and the flaw.

Subsequent authors, such as Robert Havighurst and Malcolm Knowles, believe that those who plan learning experiences for adults should take care to relate central life challenges to the learning events that adults face.

Getting It Done

Chapter 2 focused on theories of learning. Here are some questions to help you develop a mindset for the application of these theories:

Consider how applications of learning theories may influence what you do in your role as a learning professional. Can you list some theories that you use, even if unthinkingly?

What theories of learning have you applied?

1. ____

   ____

2. ____

   ____

How have those theories of learning influenced what you do as a learning professional?

1. ____

   ____

2. ____

   ____

3

Leveraging Adult Learner Differences

What's Inside This Chapter

In this chapter, you'll learn:

- How *adult learning* is defined
- What assumptions about adult learning are important for learning professionals
- How the assumptions about adult learning affect training
- What the so-called "seven intelligences" are and how they affect learning
- Which adult characteristics affect adult learning
- Aspects of brain chemistry and physiology as they affect adult learning.

Adult learning concerns, not surprisingly, how adults learn. But the term *adult* actually has more than one meaning. In one sense, adults may be understood as "mentally mature" people. In a different sense, the word *adult* may also be understood to mean those who are beyond the traditional school ages of 7 to 21. They are usually employed. *Workplace learning* is a specialized area within adult learning that focuses on how people learn in workplace settings. The theories and practice of adult learning build on what is known about learning generally, an issue examined in the previous chapter. But adult learning is also based on theory and practice arising from the specialized study of adults and what makes them special as a group of learners.

How Often Do Adults Participate in Learning?

Adults do not consistently participate in learning, either formal (planned) or informal (unplanned), throughout their life spans. Generally, younger and more highly educated workers are more likely to participate in learning efforts of all kinds than their older, or less-educated, counterparts. See Exhibits 3-1 and 3-2 for statistics about adult participation in planned and unplanned learning experiences. Exhibit 3-3 lists common reasons why adults do not participate in educational or training events.

What Assumptions of Adult Learning Are Important for Learning Professionals?

Several important assumptions about adult learners are worth emphasizing. These assumptions guide many aspects of adult learning situations. Generally, these principles may be categorized as making assumptions about adults as learners, motivating adult learners, planning instruction for adults, working with groups of adults, working with individual adult learners, helping learners transfer what they learned, and considering the barriers faced by adults in learning.

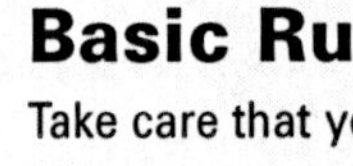

Basic Rule 4

Take care that you do not assume that all adults have the same characteristics. Some adults do not share the general characteristics that are widely attributed to adult learners. Indeed, the trend is to consider individual characteristics and learning styles. Still, it is important for you to have a fundamental understanding of adult learning theory as presented in this section.

Exhibit 3-1: Percentage of Adults Who Participated in Adult Education, By Type of Educational Activity and Selected Adult Characteristics: 2004-2005

Characteristic	Number of adults (thousands)	Any formal adult education	Formal adult education activities						
			ESL classes	Basic skills/GED classes	Part-time college degree program[1]	Part-time vocational degree/diploma program[2]	Apprentice-ship	Work-related courses	Personal-interest courses
Total	211,607	44	1	1	4	1	1	27	21
Age									
16 to 24 years	25,104	53	2	6	9	2	3	21	27
25 to 34 years	38,784	52	2	2	7	2	3	32	22
35 to 44 years	42,890	49	1	1	4	1	1	34	22
45 to 54 years	41,840	48	#	#	3	1	1	37	20
55 to 64 years	29,068	40	#	#	1	1	#	27	21
65 years or older	33,922	23	#	#	#	#	#	5	19
Sex									
Male	101,596	41	1	1	4	1	2	24	18
Female	110,011	47	1	1	4	1	1	29	24
Race/ethnicity									
White, non-Hispanic	146,614	46	#	1	4	1	1	29	22
Black, non-Hispanic	23,467	46	#	2	4	1	2	27	24
Hispanic	26,101	38	6	3	4	1	2	17	15
Asian or Pacific Islander, non-Hispanic	7,080	44	2	1!	6	1!	1!	24	23
Other race, non-Hispanic.	8,346	39	#	1	4	1	2	23	20

(continued on next page)

Exhibit 3-1: Percentage of Adults Who Participated in Adult Education, By Type of Educational Activity and Selected Adult Characteristics: 2004-2005 (continued)

Characteristic	Number of adults (thousands)	Any formal adult education	Formal adult education activities						
			ESL classes	Basic skills/GED classes	Part-time college degree program[1]	Part-time vocational degree/diploma program[2]	Apprentice-ship	Work-related courses	Personal-interest courses
Highest education level completed									
Less than a high school diploma/equivalent	31,018	22	2	7	#	1	1	4	11
High school diploma/equivalent	64,334	33	1	1	2	1	2	17	16
Some college/vocational/associate's degree	58,545	51	1	#	6	2	1	31	25
Bachelor's degree	37,244	60	#	#	6	1	#	44	29
Graduate or professional education or degree	20,466	66	1!	#	7	1	1!	51	30
Household income									
$20,000 or less	34,670	28	1	2	2	1	2	11	16
$20,001 to $35,000	35,839	36	2	2	4	1	1	18	17
$35,001 to $50,000	33,376	42	2!	1	2	1	1	23	22
$50,001 to $75,000	47,114	48	#	#	5	1	1	33	21
$75,001 or more	60,607	58	1	1	5	2	1	39	27

Estimate rounds to 0 or 0 cases in sample.

! Interpret data with caution; coefficient of variation is 50 percent or more.

1 Includes those enrolled only part-time in college or university degree or certificate programs or those enrolled through a combination of part-time and full-time enrollments in the 12 months prior to the interview.

2 Includes those enrolled only part-time in vocational or technical diploma, degree, certificate programs or those enrolled through a combination of part-time and full-time enrollments in the 12 months prior to the interview.

Source: http://nces.ed/gov/pubs2006/adulted/tables/table_1.asp

Exhibit 3-2: Number and Percentage of Adults Who Reported Participating in Informal Learning Activities for Personal Interest, By Type of Educational Activity and Selected Adult Characteristics: 2004-2005

			Type of informal learning activities for personal interest				
Characteristic	**Number of adults (thousands)**	**Any informal learning activities**	**Computers, CD-ROM, and Internet**	**Books, manuals, audio tapes, videos, or TV**	**Magazines or other publications**	**Clubs or groups**	**Conventions or conferences**
Total	211,607	70	28	47	53	20	23
Age							
16 to 24 years	25,104	69	29	42	45	18	25
25 to 34 years	38,784	70	33	49	50	20	25
35 to 44 years	42,890	73	32	51	56	21	23
45 to 54 years	41,840	73	31	51	59	23	27
55 to 64 years	29,068	70	27	47	56	21	23
65 years or older	33,922	64	15	38	49	17	17
Sex							
Male	101,596	71	30	49	55	17	26
Female	110,011	70	26	45	52	24	21
Race/ethnicity							
White, non-Hispanic	146,614	73	29	48	57	22	25
Black, non-Hispanic	23,467	65	26	46	44	18	20
Hispanic	26,101	57	20	37	38	14	16
Asian or Pacific Islander, non-Hispanic	7,080	78	33	47	57	14	20
Other race, non-Hispanic.	8,346	74	35	55	57	26	28

(continued on next page)

Exhibit 3-2: Number and Percentage of Adults Who Reported Participating in Informal Learning Activities for Personal Interest, By Type of Educational Activity and Selected Adult Characteristics: 2004-2005 (continued)

Characteristic	Number of adults (thousands)	Any informal learning activities	Type of informal learning activities for personal interest				
			Computers, CD-ROM, and Internet	Books, manuals, audio tapes, videos, or TV	Magazines or other publications	Clubs or groups	Conventions or conferences
Highest education level completed							
Less than a high school diploma/equivalent	31,017	46	8	27	27	6	11
High school diploma/ equivalent	64,334	63	22	40	46	14	18
Some college/vocational/ associate's degree	58,545	79	35	53	62	27	28
Bachelor's degree	37,244	79	37	56	64	24	30
Graduate or professional education or degree	20,466	89	42	66	70	34	36
Household income							
$20,000 or less	34,670	59	19	37	37	14	13
$20,001 to $35,000	35,839	67	21	45	47	16	20
$35,001 to $50,000	33,376	71	27	46	51	18	22
$50,001 to $75,000	47,114	71	31	47	56	22	24
$75,001 or more	60,607	78	35	55	65	26	32
Employment status							
Employed full-time	106,388	72	32	50	56	20	27
Employed part-time	27,090	78	33	52	58	25	29
Unemployed and looking for work	9,941	67	29	49	41	16	16
Not in the labor force	68,187	65	19	40	49	19	17

Source: http://nces.ed.gov/pubs2006/adulted/tables/table_17.asp

Exhibit 3-3: Typical Obstacles to Adult Participation in Education and Training Experiences

Adults are less likely to participate in education and training

- the lower their level of schooling
- the lower their level of educational attainment
- the lower the socio-economic status
- when they cannot get away from work or get supervisory approval
- when they face social pressures from home or family not to participate
- when they do not perceive that education or training will benefit them
- when they are unfamiliar with how to apply what they learn
- when they are unfamiliar with what educational or learning opportunities are available
- when they do not have time
- when they do not have the resources (such as transportation) to get to the opportunity
- when they lack child care or other support systems to help them participate in education or training.

Assumptions About Adults As Learners. Well-known author and theorist Malcolm Knowles stated that most adult learners are autonomous. Most of them want to take charge of their lives, their learning, and their careers. They are *self-directed*, meaning they are willing to initiate their own learning efforts when they see the need to do so. When the moment is right because adults are encountering a personal situation that prompts them to learn—what is called a *teachable moment*—adults see the need to learn and are highly motivated to do so. Such teachable moments occur when adults are confronting a work or life problem or feel that they are about to face such a problem. As a simple example, adults become highly motivated to learn about Japan just before they go there; similarly, they become interested in learning about babies just before they become parents.

Self-directed learning does not, however, mean that adults prefer to learn individually or in isolation. Instead, studies of such learning indicate that learners may draw on at least 10 other resources as they pursue individualized learning projects. Many adults prefer group interaction to less social settings for learning.

In recent years, authorities of adult learning have noted the rise of so-called free agent learners. Free agent learners are aggressive about pursuing what they want to know and will draw on many sources to find out what they need. Some quip that free agent learners are "self-directed learners on steroids." Think about how people conduct a search online, filter through many websites, and zero in on just what it is that they think they need. This aggressive approach typifies the way a free agent learner pursues a learning task.

Few adults want to hear about history, theory, or background when they are motivated to learn; rather, they want to build on their own wealth of knowledge and experience. In short, they come to learning with their own sense of identity and sense of what they already know. Adults usually find it difficult to learn if the learning clashes with their values, beliefs, or previous experience.

Assumptions About Motivating Adult Learners. Adults are motivated to learn for different reasons. These motivators may generally be categorized into six groups:

- *Build social networks*: Make new acquaintances.
- *Meet expectations*: Comply with what supervisors or others want the learners to do.
- *Advance in their careers*: Prepare for, or meet, promotion requirements.
- *Be stimulated*: Find escape and adventure through learning.
- *Help others*: Meet perceived social obligations to other people.
- *Learn for its own sake*: Enjoy the free play of the mind in pursuit of knowledge and skills.

Efforts to motivate learners will work best when they are tied to the appropriate reasons that attracted the learners to participate in a learning situation.

An especially effective technique is to ask learners why they want to learn. This can be done by questionnaire or email before they participate in a learning event,

Basic Rule 5

Learners set out to learn for different reasons. Their reasons for learning should be considered in the design of learning experiences. Do this by surfacing what learners want from the learning experience early on in that experience.

or it can be done at the outset of training by posing the question to the learner group and flipcharting what they said. Then the trainer should ensure that learners' expectations are met. One way to do that is to conclude a training session by reviewing the flipcharted list that learners provided and ensuring that each problem they wanted to solve has been addressed in the training.

Assumptions About Planning Instruction for Adults. Adults do not like general learning experiences; rather, they prefer focused learning that centers around how to apply key ideas, principles, or the experience of others. Older adults may take longer to acquire new knowledge or skills, because they tend to be more careful about learning something so as to do it right. They are less willing than younger people to experiment without careful planning.

Adults invest their egos heavily in what they learn and how they learn. They do not like to make mistakes that make them appear stupid, foolish, or incompetent. For this reason, the learning environment should provide support and encouragement. Young adults, who grew up with web access, are quite willing to learn online. But older adults are sometimes less willing or less desirous of learning experiences that minimize face-to-face interaction.

Assumptions About Working With Groups of Adults. The setting in which adults learn must be comfortable to them both physically and psychologically. For that reason, adults do not favor sitting on hard chairs through long, boring lectures; rather, they prefer active and interactive settings in which to learn—stimulating, but safe psychologically. Adults come to group learning events with expectations about what will happen, and the learning process works most effectively when their expectations are surfaced and addressed.

Adults generally respond best to learning situations in which facilitators pose questions, provide just enough information to serve as a foundation for discussion, give learners the chance to participate in the discussion, and yield opportunities for them to interact with their peers. Consequently, facilitation skills are of crucial importance to teachers or trainers of adults.

Of greatest importance is knowledge of how to pose open questions, typically understood to mean questions beginning with *who*, *what*, *when*, *where*, *why*, or *how*. (Closed questions, in contrast, begin with *is*, *was*, *did*, or *have*.)

In groups, some adults tend to be more participative than others. A typical challenge for facilitators is to seek balanced participation. They can do this by calling on otherwise silent people or going around the group and asking each person to offer a comment or an answer to a question.

Adults typically need opportunities to practice or apply new knowledge or skills. That means it is often wise to ask groups of learners to engage in open-ended activities in which they must come up with a group answer to a difficult problem, analyze case studies, participate in role plays, or take part in any learning activity that encourages interaction.

Assumptions About Working With Individual Adult Learners. Individual learning efforts often tap theories and practice of coaching and mentoring. Those working with individuals have the advantage of being able to find out what motivates individuals and direct attention to those motivators. Often just a few questions can help a facilitator in a one-on-one learning situation determine how much an individual is interested in building social networks, meeting supervisory expectations, advancing their careers, finding adventure, helping others, or learning for the sake of learning.

Assumptions About Helping Learners Transfer What They Learned. A topic of perennial interest to trainers is how to increase transfer of training, sometimes called *transfer of learning*. It is commonly understood that less than 8 percent of off-the-job training transfers back to the job in changed behavior. That means each dollar spent on training yields only eight cents of impact.

There are several reasons why adults do not transfer what they learned. One big reason is short-term memory loss. As mentioned in the previous chapter, adults forget about 80 percent of what they hear within 48 hours. Hence, to increase memory retention, trainers must find ways to make it easy for learners to apply what they learned. Techniques to do so may include giving them job aids (such as checklists) or practical tools that they can use immediately.

Another reason why adults do not transfer what they learn is that supervisors and co-workers are seldom in the same training session. When workers return to their jobs from training, their supervisors and co-workers may not support their efforts to apply what they learned. In fact, they may even ridicule such efforts. ("Where did you learn that? From trainers? What do they know!") Group norms, the unspoken ways that people relate to each other in small groups, influence how much people are willing to apply what they learned. To increase transfer of learning, trainers must consider ways to help impact on-the-job norms.

Here are a few simple tips to increase the transfer of learning:

- Give participants memorable instruction, since adults tend to remember interesting stories more than rules, principles, theories, or descriptions.
- Appeal to as many senses as possible, since learners will tend to remember better when appeals are made to a range of senses, such as sight, hearing, touch, and smell.
- Relate training to what learners already know, purposely working to build on it.
- Identify the on-the-job problems that learners face, and make an effort to help them solve those problems.

Considering the Barriers Faced by Adults in Learning. Adults face many barriers that hold them back from learning as they may need or want to. Such barriers center on lack of time, money, self-esteem, interest, management support, scheduling difficulties, life responsibilities that may conflict with learning opportunities, care of others (such as children or elderly parents), and transportation.

It is particularly effective to find out what barriers adults perceive in their learning process. Trainers should simply ask, usually at the outset of training or at the end, what barriers the learners perceive may affect their ability to apply what they learn and what organizational leaders can do to knock down those barriers.

What Are the Seven Intelligences, and How Do They Affect Adult Learning?

Intelligence is a very old notion. Efforts to measure it have been numerous. But intelligence can be, and should be, regarded as more than just limited views of cognition (knowing). Harvard professor Howard Gardner first introduced the idea that intelligence is a concept that has many components. He calls these components "multiple intelligences," which are described in his now-famous book *Frames of Mind* (Gardner, 1983).

Gardner believed that the first challenge confronting educators or trainers is to get over the notion that intelligence means only one thing. It is a higher-order construct with many facets. Once educators and trainers grasp the full complexity of what intelligence really means, they can start to use that more sophisticated knowledge to help people learn more effectively.

Gardner initially listed seven types of intelligence. Each intelligence can be used to appeal to different dimensions of an individual's ability to learn. Gardner further believed that intelligence is contextualized—that is, grounded in the setting in which the intelligence is to be enacted. It is also distributed in that people know not only what is in their heads but also tap resources (other people, tools, sources of information) to perform.

Verbal/linguistic intelligence is the ability to make effective use of words, whether in writing or in speaking. The skills associated with this type of intelligence includes remembering facts, figures, and other information. It also includes communicating about words and persuading other people to help in the learning process. Poets have a highly developed form of this intelligence.

Musical intelligence has to do with an individual's sensitivity to such musical components as melody, pitch, and rhythm. Composers have a highly developed form of this intelligence.

Logical or mathematical intelligence centers around an individual's ability to use numbers and reasoning. It includes being able to perceive cause-and-effect relationships and the ability to predict what may happen. Scientists have a highly developed form of this intelligence.

Spatial and visual intelligence focuses on awareness of color, lines, shapes, spatial relationships, and form. Individuals who can use this intelligence effectively use visual cues and spatial relationships. They rely on graphics. Artists have a highly developed form of this intelligence.

Bodily or kinesthetic intelligence is an awareness of how to use the body for communicating ideas, expressing feelings, or solving problems. Individuals who can dance, for instance, reflect a highly developed sense of this type of intelligence. They use speed, balance, hand-and-eye coordination, and bodily flexibility. Professional athletes, surgeons, and movie actors have a highly developed form of this intelligence.

Interpersonal intelligence focuses on awareness of other people's emotions, values, and beliefs. Those possessing interpersonal intelligence are keenly aware of how other people feel, know what motivates them, and can feel empathy. Psychiatrists and teachers have highly developed forms of this intelligence.

Intrapersonal intelligence focuses on one's awareness of self. People who possess intrapersonal intelligence know themselves. They are aware of their own strengths, weaknesses, feelings, beliefs, values, and emotions. They know how they compare to other people. Individuals who have heeded Socrates' admonition to "know thyself" have a highly developed form of this intelligence.

Awareness of these types of intelligence is all well and good. But how is this knowledge applied? Trainers familiar with these intelligences use them to facilitate the learning process.

Tips to encourage learners to use these intelligences may include the following approaches (see http://members.tripod.com/jrmeads_515/intelleg.htm):

Verbal/linguistic intelligence

To encourage this intelligence, ask learners to

- take notes
- listen to discussions
- participate in panel discussions
- tell a story
- listen to a story
- listen to an audiotape
- participate in a teleconference
- conduct a benchmarking study.

Musical intelligence

To encourage this intelligence, ask learners to

- sing
- listen to music
- play music
- clap in tempo
- chant
- develop a slogan, motto, or name (as advertisers do).

Logical or mathematical intelligence

To encourage this intelligence, ask learners to

- participate in solving puzzles
- play games
- detect words within other words
- follow simple word patterns
- prepare a presentation to explain an idea step by step
- develop a budget
- prepare a forecast.

Spatial and visual intelligence

To encourage this intelligence, ask learners to

- prepare a chart
- watch a movie
- draw or paint something
- use art to express something.

Bodily or kinesthetic intelligence

To encourage this intelligence, ask learners to

- dance
- stand up and take part in some kind of activity
- walk around (as in an icebreaker to collect information)
- demonstrate a skill requiring physical effort
- take part in adventure learning (ropes or similar activities)
- participate in a field trip
- cook
- undertake a do-it-yourself project, such as fix a car.

Interpersonal intelligence

To encourage this intelligence, ask learners to

- teach each other (peer learning)
- participate in a board game
- participate in group problem-solving
- participate in action learning
- solve a problem in a group setting
- conduct creative brainstorming or idea generation
- participate on a task force or committee
- shadow someone to watch what he or she does
- give advice to other people about what they should do to solve a problem or meet a challenge.

Intrapersonal intelligence

To encourage this intelligence, ask learners to

- participate in a full-circle, multi-rater (360-degree) assessment
- keep a personal learning journal

- use self-reflection questionnaires or interest inventories (such as Myers-Briggs)
- share how they feel
- set goals.

Awareness of these intelligences can be most useful in helping trainers of adults to involve learners in the learning process. After all, most adults want to be active and not passively rely on instructors to learn. Awareness of multiple intelligences can also help trainers plan activities that will tap these multiple intelligences, thereby enriching the learning process.

Since *Frames of Mind* was first published, Howard Gardner has continued his work on multiple intelligences. In 1996 he proposed an eighth intelligence, ***naturalist intelligence***, which centers on sensitivity to nature and awareness of a person's place in it and relationship to it. This could emerge as being more important at a time when "thinking green" has grown more popular as awareness of global warming has led to concerns about each person's "carbon footprint." Gardner has also suggested that a ninth could be possible, which he calls *existentialist intelligence* (the ability to reflect on the meaning of life and death). Other authors have extended his thinking by adding *emotional intelligence* (Goleman, 1997).

Adult Characteristics That Affect Adult Learning

Adults differ from children in the simple, and obvious, sense that they are older. And that is important, because there are fundamental differences between children and adults stemming simply from age. Children have few, if any, age-related problems. But as adults age, it is a well-known fact that their senses of sight and hearing decline. Adults also experience changes in how well they remember things and how willing they are to participate in planned learning experiences such as group training.

Age-Related Differences in Hearing. Nearly one in three U.S. adults between ages 65 and 75 experiences some form of hearing loss. About 1.5 of every three U.S. adults 75 years or over also experience hearing loss. "We are born with a set of sensory cells, and, at about age 18, we slowly start to lose them," according to Hinrich Staecker, M.D., Ph.D., director of the otology and neurotology program at the University of Maryland Medical Center in Baltimore. But because age-related hearing loss, called *presbycusis*, progresses so slowly, most people don't notice any changes until well after age 50 (Rados, 2005). There is no one reason that hearing loss occurs; rather, there are many.

The point to understand is that adults—particularly older adults—may need help to hear as they participate in planned learning experiences. Loss of hearing does occur with age, presenting an obstacle for adult learners as they grow older.

Age-Related Differences in Seeing. According to the National Eye Institute,"With the aging of the population, the number of Americans with major eye diseases is increasing, and vision loss is becoming a major public health problem. By the year 2020, the number of people who are blind or have low vision is projected to increase substantially. Blindness or low vision affects 3.3 million Americans age 40 and over, or one in 28" (*Vision Loss*, 2004).

So what? As the population ages, vision loss will pose a major challenge for individuals and organizations alike if they are to help people maintain their skills and learn effectively. Trainers will need to be vigilant about this problem.

Age-Related Differences in Memory. While people may tell bad jokes about memory loss and old age, the reality is that memory loss is not solely dependent on age or even necessarily affected by it. According to C.E. Barber (2005), "out of 42.7 million Americans over 60, loss of memory for recent events affects 7 to 10 percent (3 to 4 million). For some, recall is just slowed down. For others, memory impairment becomes both noticeable and troublesome."

The conclusions to be drawn from age-memory research are these:

- There are three types of memory—sensory, short-term, and long-term. Age-related problems may actually stem from sensory loss because people cannot see or hear what they are learning.
- Older adults may have more fragile short-term memory than younger adults.

Age does not have a relationship to long-term memory so far as research has shown.

Age-Related Differences in Learning. Although there are elements of "wear and tear," the idea of "use it or lose it" seems best in regard to learning as people age. Having concluded this, it seems useful to give advice about how we can better cope with the aging process. Since the nervous system undergoes complex changes late in life, it is best not to alter it further. Alcohol and certain drugs that act on the central nervous system can impair cognitive abilities (Selkoe, 1996). Scientists, however, may be able to develop effective drugs that stop some of the effects of the aging process.

Environment is critical to consider in the aging process. A study that ended in 1994 assessed the mental abilities of more than 5,000 adults (Rosenzweig & Bennett, 1996). The study's results revealed that there are several key environmental factors that reduce risk of mental decline as people age. First is having work that involves high complexity and low routine. Second is maintaining intact families. Third is participating in continuing education activities and social events.

Age-Related Differences in Learning Disabilities. According to the Foundation for People with Learning Disabilities, about 2 percent of the U.S. population has a learning disability. The number of people over age 60 with a learning disability is expected to grow by 36 percent from 2001 to 2021. Nearly one in three people who have a learning disability claim that they do not maintain contact with any friends or family.

There are many kinds of learning disabilities. Perhaps best known is dyslexia, the tendency for the brain to scramble the order of printed words. But there are many others, some not so well documented, understood, or commonly diagnosed. Trainers of the future must become aware of these possible learning disabilities and be prepared to make reasonable accommodations so that learners can keep their knowledge, skills, and attitudes up to date and can receive training despite the learning disabilities from which they suffer.

Aspects of Brain Chemistry and Physiology Affecting Adult Learning

One of the most exciting developments in recent years to affect education and training is the emergence of *brain neuroscience* or *learning science*, which is the study of how the brain works, both chemically and physiologically. The implications of learning science for training are profound, and researchers have only scratches the surface of understanding what makes the brain work, how to tap into knowledge of the brain to improve the learning process, and how age affects the brain and the learning process. While space is limited here to discuss this complex topic, the goal is to introduce some important information about how learning science affects what is known about the brain and the learning process, how an understanding of the brain may influence training practice, and how age affects the human brain's capacity to learn.

How Learning Science Affects What Is Known About the Brain and the Learning Process. The human brain is a marvelous creation. And yet, according to some estimates, computers will have reached the ability to simulate human thought by about 2020, if present trends continue (Moravec, 1997). By 1997, IBM's Deep Blue Supercomputer was good enough to best reigning World Chess Champion Garry Kasparov.

About the size of a cauliflower head, the brain regulates body chemistry, controls the body's movement, handles automatic functions such as breathing, and allows human beings to think and feel. Composed of about 100 billion cells called neurons, the brain functions through electrochemical signals. Most people know that the brain consists of such basic parts as a medulla (at the top of the spinal cord), the cerebellum, and cerebrum or cortex. The medulla regulates automatic body functions such as heart rate and breathing; the cerebellum helps coordinate movement of the limbs; and the cerebrum is the center of thought and of important senses. There are, of course, many other parts to the brain, all commonly thought to control different human functions. See Exhibit 3-4 for a picture of the brain. For more on parts of the brain, see http://en.wikipedia.org/wiki/List_of_regions_in_the_human_brain.

The brain is also commonly divided by a big fold in the middle that creates a right side and a left side. These are associated with different aspects of human beings. The left brain controls reason and analysis; the right brain is the center of creative thinking and feeling. The left side of the body is wired to the right side of the brain; the right side of the body is wired to the left side of the brain. Roger Sperry conducted the groundbreaking research on the two parts of the brain. He conducted experiments with an individual who lost half of his brain. The left side of the brain tends to be fact oriented, relies on logic, uses words, and is present and past oriented. The right side of the brain relies on feelings, focuses on the big picture (not details), and is present and future oriented.

Awareness of brain architecture provides only a partial understanding of how the brain works. Since the brain functions through electrochemical signals, brain chemistry is essential to an awareness of how the brain works. The study of brain chemicals is often associated with brain neurochemistry. (For a more complete discussion of this topic, see http://en.wikipedia.org/wiki/Neurochemistry.)

A few examples of neurochemicals include

- dopamine, a neurotransmitter that affects emotional functions
- serotonin, which affects moods and sleep

- acetylcholine, which assists motor function
- nitric oxide, a gas that can also serve as a neurotransmitter.

How an Understanding of the Brain May Influence Training Practice. Trainers should remain attuned to advances in brain chemistry and physiology so as to be aware of how that information may increase the efficiency and effectiveness of training. People exercise their bodies to get in shape. They can also exercise their brains to attune their attention, memory, mood, sleep, and even their learning. According to a research study of 700 Chicago residents with an average age of 80, published in an online edition of *Neurology*, researchers found that older people who engage in stimulating mental activities, such as chess or reading newspapers, can reduce the

Exhibit 3-4: Different Parts of the Brain Commonly Thought to Control Different Human Functions

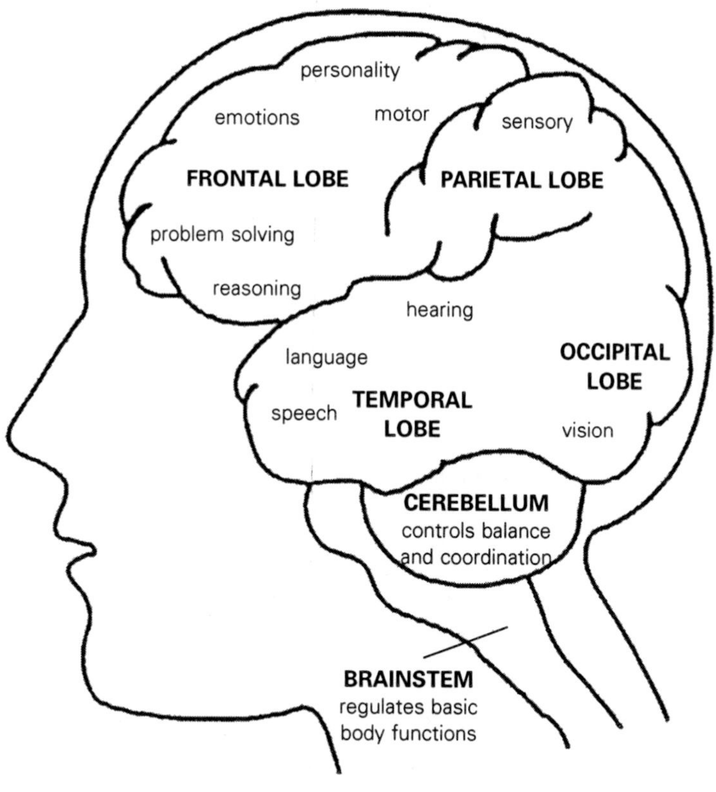

Source: http://www.state.sc.us/ddsn/pubs/head/brain.gif. Used by permission.

risk of Alzheimer's. So, there is reason to conclude that mental exercise can reduce the risk of developing dementia in older people.

Consequently, adults who engage in planned training are being mentally stimulated. This can also reduce the risk of developing dementia. Unfortunately, research also shows that older adults are much less likely to participate in training or other planned learning events than younger people.

According to author Ronald Gross in "Your Learning and Your Brain: Five Ways to Enhance Your Learning" (http://adulted.about.com/od/learningstyles/a/brain.htm), awareness of how the brain works can influence learning in five specific ways. First, each person's brain is unique. Just as faces are different, so are brains. Individuals have different learning styles. Second, the brain requires significant challenge. People become frustrated if the learning challenge is too great, but become bored and indifferent if the learning challenge is too easy. Third, the brain is a physical organ and is therefore subject to the same influences as any other organ. Excessive heat, light, bad food, and other environmental influences can impact the quality of the brain's operations. Fourth, the brain's ability to learn is influenced by emotions and feelings. What is learned best is associated with significant emotional events, such as extraordinary successes or miserable failures. Fifth and finally, as discussed earlier in this chapter, we each possess multiple intelligences or special mental strengths.

How Age Affects the Human Brain's Capacity to Learn. As the U.S. population ages—and, indeed, the global population is also aging—interest is growing in how age may affect the human brain's capacity to learn as older workers become an important resource to meet possible future talent shortages. While we have all heard that "you can't teach an old dog new tricks," that old saying is just plain wrong. Few differences distinguish young and old people. While older people—those beyond traditional retirement age of 65—do tend to require more time to master new skills, that is not because their brains are not as agile as younger people. Rather, the difference tends to center on the extra care that older people take to "get it right." They do not wish to lose face by performing badly and therefore tend to be more cautious in trying out new things.

A key issue in understanding the difference between younger and older workers is the difference between crystallized and fluid intelligence. It was psychologist Raymond Cattell who first described crystallized and fluid intelligence. His theory was later refined through work with John Horn. *Fluid intelligence* refers to an individual's ability to see relationships without previous practice or knowledge; *crystallized intelligence* refers to an individual's learning from experience. Fluid intelligence centers around thinking and reasoning abstractly and solving problems; crystallized intelligence includes reading ability. Generally speaking, both types of intelligence increase from childhood through adolescence. However, fluid intelligence reaches a peak in adolescence and then declines after age 30. Crystallized intelligence never peaks and grows through all phases of adulthood. As a result, younger adults tend to do best with problem solving and trying out new experiences, while older adults do best by building on their experience.

Individuals sustain the ability to learn effectively unless they become prone to diseases affecting age—most notably Alzheimer's disease, a brain disorder named for the German medical doctor Alois Alzheimer. It is a progressive disease that destroys brain cells, creating problems with memory, thinking, and behavior. According to the Alzheimer's Association, (1) as many as 5.2 million people in the United States are afflicted with Alzheimer's; (2) 10 million Baby Boomers will develop Alzheimer's in their lifetime; (3) every 71 seconds, someone develops Alzheimer's; (4) Alzheimer's is the seventh-leading cause of death; and (5) the direct and indirect costs of Alzheimer's and other dementias to Medicare, Medicaid, and businesses amount to more than $148 billion each year (http://www.alz.org/alzheimers_disease_facts_figures.asp).

There are other dementia that can affect people in old age and can affect their learning abilities. *Dementia,* a term referring to loss of memory and other mental abilities, interferes with daily life and is caused by physical changes in the brain. While Alzheimer's is the most common, accounting for about 50 to 70 percent of cases of age-related brain disorders, other dementia include the following:

- *Mild Cognitive Impairment (MCI)*: This is a condition in which people have problems with memory, language, or other mental functions sufficiently to be noticed by others, but not enough to affect their ability to function independently on a daily basis.
- *Vascular Dementia*: Caused by diminished blood flow to the brain, it is the second most common type of dementia. It develops when impaired blood flow to parts of the brain deprives cells of food and oxygen.
- *Mixed Dementia*: This results when Alzheimer's and vascular dementia occur at the same time.

- *Dementia with Lewy Bodies*: Characterized by abnormal deposits of a protein called alpha-synuclein that form inside the brain's nerve cells, it results in memory problems, confusion, and other cognitive problems. The deposits are called "Lewy Bodies" because Lewy was the scientist who first identified them.
- *Parkinson's Disease*: Beginning with problems affecting bodily movement, Parkinson's can lead to difficulties with speech, movement, and muscle control.
- *Frontotemporal Dementia*: A rare disorder affecting the frontal and temporal lobes of the brain, it presents faster than Alzheimer's. Initial symptoms include changes in personality and judgment, as well as rude or off-color remarks.
- *Creutzfeldt-Jakob Disease (CJD)*: A rare and frequently fatal disorder that afflicts nearly one in 1 million people per year globally, it typically affects individuals older than age 60. Its initial symptoms involve impaired memory, thinking, and reasoning. It can include also changes in personality and behavior, depression, and agitation.
- *Normal Pressure Hydrocephalus*: A rare disorder caused by an inability of fluid surrounding the brain and spinal cord to drain normally, it leads to loss of bladder control and mental decline.
- *Huntington's Disease*: A fatal brain disorder, it prompts problems with balance and coordination, personality changes, and leads to trouble with memory and concentration.
- *Wernicke-Korsakoff Syndrome*: A brain disorder caused by a deficiency of vitamin B-1, it leads to gaps in memory and problems in learning new information. People have a tendency to make up information that they cannot remember. It is accompanied by lack of coordination and unsteadiness.

Trainers should learn more about these dementia, since an aging population makes it more likely that such disorders will surface increasingly and may affect the ability of older workers to learn (Rothwell, Sterns, Spokus, & Reaser, 2008). Trainers should be prepared to spot possible symptoms and refer individuals who may need help to proper medical professionals.

Getting It Done

In chapter 3, you learned about how to define *adult learning,* assumptions commonly made about adult learning, and how those assumptions about adult learning may affect training. You also learned what is meant by the "seven intelligences" and their impact on learning, which adult characteristics affect adult learning, and aspects of brain chemistry as it affects learning.

Consider the following questions:

1. How would you define an adult?

   ____

   ____

   ____

2. How would you describe what is unique about teaching adults?

   ____

   ____

   ____

3. How would you describe what might be unique about teaching older adults?

   ____

   ____

   ____

If it is true that the best way to learn something is to be required to teach it, prepare a brief presentation on the topics presented in this chapter, and be prepared to share it with your colleagues.

4

Engaging Boomer, Gen X, and Gen Y Learners

What's Inside This Chapter

In this chapter, you'll learn:

- What a *self-directed* learner is and how it differs from a *free agent* learner
- What is known, or at least speculated, about generational differences among adult learners
- How the unique characteristics of different generations of adult learners may influence their expectations about learning.

The Generational Differences

Much has been written about generational differences among learners. These differences may be a factor in shaping learning situations and addressing the needs of various adult learners. One size does not fit all, and that is especially true of learning events. Not all learners are identical. While there is always the danger of stereotyping learners, it seems clear that different generations have had exposure to different experiences as they grew up. For instance, those at retirement age right now grew up before television was popular. They learned to read and used reading and writing as entertainment. Some experienced a world at an early age in which "high tech" meant the radio. Baby Boomers grew up with television. It shaped their expectations, leading some to believe that all complex problems could be quickly solved within 30 minutes or one hour—the length of a typical television show. Their reading and writing skills were not as advanced as those of their parents. Those born since 1985 grew up near the Internet, and many had at least some exposure to it before leaving their formal schooling. Others had much more exposure to it and came to rely on such gadgets as cell phones, video recorders, iPods, game players, and computers. To them, huge amounts of information are available but require filtering.

This chapter provides an overview of some generational differences that exist among today's learner populations and offers suggestions on how trainers may appeal to these different groups.

What Is a *Self-Directed Learner,* and What Is a *Free Agent Learner*?

The term *self-directed learner* does not have one uniform definition. And yet a common view is that most adult learners are self-directed.

According to Huey B. Long in "Skills for Self-Directed Learning" (http://faculty-staff.ou.edu/L/Huey.B.Long-1/Articles/sd/selfdirected.html), "Self-directed learning is a purposive mental process, usually accompanied and supported by behavioral activities involved in the identification and searching out of information. The learner consciously accepts the responsibility to make decisions about goals and effort, and is, hence, one's own learning change agent." Learners have the stamina and fortitude, both cognitively and personally, to take responsibility for their own learning and assertively pursue what is needed to help them solve problems they face or goals they seek to achieve. Mardziah Abdullah (2001) defines self-directed learners as "responsible owners and managers of their own learning process" (p. 1). They know how to manage themselves and monitor their own learning process.

Individuals can be trained to be more self-directed, and their skills as self-directed learners can be developed. Long developed a list of self-directed learning skills, which are presented in Exhibit 4-1. Use that list to assess how well individuals or even teams may be considered self-directed. Supplement that list with the additional features of self-directed learners appearing in Exhibit 4-2.

Exhibit 4-1: Six Skills for Self-Directed Learning

According to Huey B. Long, the skills of a self-directed learner are as follows:

Personality Traits

Some of the personality traits are

- self-confidence
- inner directed
- achievement motivated.

General Skills

Assuming the individual has a moderate allocation of the identified personality attributes, at least six kinds of cognitive skills appear to be particularly important in successful self-directed learning. They are as follows:

- Goal-setting skills
- Processing skills
- Other cognitive skills
- Some competence or aptitude in the topic or a closely related area
- Decision-making skills
- Self-awareness.

1) Goal-Setting Skills

Unfortunately many individuals have not learned how to determine what is important and then how to select from among alternative possibilities—or even imagine possibilities that have not been given to them by authority figures. These individuals have become accustomed to having questions and problems identified for them rather than developing the cognitive ability to engage in problem identification and problem posing. As a consequence, they may also have limited observational skills that inhibit their ability to determine what is important in their learning environment. Therefore, some effort is often required to develop these skills before a person becomes a successful self-directed learner. Thus, when working with people with little experience in self-directed learning, careful attention should be given to helping them to imagine possible outcomes of the results of their learning, then encouraging them to know how and why to choose from among multiple desirable goals.

2) Information-Processing Skills

Even though strong reading ability is often identified with successful self-directed learners, there are other information-processing skills that are also important. From the available research, it is assumed that the self-directed learner is able to attend to and process information by using at least one of the following skills:

- Observing—the ability to see and do, or the ability to see and understand
- Seeing and translating—the ability to translate visual information to notes and records, or the ability to reproduce visual information graphically and relate it to existing information schemes
- Reading—the ability to read, translate, and comprehend written material
- Listening—the ability to receive and process aural information and relate it to existing information schemes.

(continued on next page)

Exhibit 4-1: Six Skills for Self-Directed Learning (continued)

3) Other Cognitive Skills

In addition to the above information-processing abilities, other cognitive skills appear to be associated with self-directed learning success. Some of these skills are

- sensory, including the ability to select from multiple sensory input, identify, and classify the sensory information
- memory, since working memory is important in the processing of information before it is assimilated into existing long-term memory
- elaboration, including the ability to take an item from working memory and process it by imaging, deducing, discriminating, generalizing, and so forth
- problem solving and problem posing.

Executive Skills

Self-directed learners are different from other-directed learners in the degree to which they can focus on information and monitor their processing and other cognitive activities. They also differ in the way they react to information. A simple illustration is found in the self-directed learner's act of reading and studying. Self-directed learners are aware of when they cease to interact with the written material and begin merely to process words. A change in behavior may be called for, and the learner may adopt a different procedure, such as note taking or drawing schemata, to refocus on the material and stay on task.

Executives skills required include

- pre-task monitoring
- using a strategy for gathering and using information
- information gathering
- self-awareness as it pertains to existing prior knowledge, personal cognitive processes, and ability to control the cognitive system
- self-monitoring
- reflection
- assimilating/accommodating.

Deep-Processing Skills

The successful self-directed learner engages in deep cognitive processing, an important activity associated with self-directed learner activities. The learner

- derives enjoyment from the activity
- searches for meaning in the information
- often personalizes the task by relating it to his or her own experience
- relates bit and parts of the information, relates evidence to conclusions, and relates the whole to previous knowledge
- develops theories and forms hypotheses.

The above deep-processing activities may be contrasted with surface processing, which includes the following characteristics:

- Learning is perceived as a task—a demand or requirement that is a necessary imposition to achieve a goal.
- Learners see aspects of parts as discrete and unrelated to each other or to other learning goals.
- Learners avoid personal or other meanings the learning activities may have.
- Learners rely on memorization, attempting to reproduce the surface of the learning task, repeating words or diagrams, and so forth rather than rephrasing or elaborating as a means of understanding.

The result of surface processing as opposed to deep processing may be similar to what Alfred North Whitehead called "inert" ideas. The content, ideas, and observations in surface processing are mere mental reproductions in the absence of active meaningful mental activity.

4) Content Competence

Some minimal level of aptitude or competence in the self-directed learning topic, or a closely related area, seems to be desirable, if not necessary. Because of limited understanding of ontological knowledge development, the premise of pre-existing or *a priori* competence is difficult to prove or disprove. But personal observations indicate that people skilled in certain areas tend to emphasize those, while avoiding topics and activities in areas in which they are less competent. For example, an individual is likely to be a more successful self-directed learner with some pre-existing awareness of fundamental vocabulary, concepts, and structure of the information. Hence, someone who knows basic arithmetic may be able to be self-directing in learning math, then algebra, then geometry, and so forth. Or someone who knows their own language may learn another language based on knowledge of the first language.

5) Decision-Making Skills

This skill category might be given a number of labels to connote "thinking" ability. Some might refer to it as being logical in thought. Others might prefer analytical. And yet others might choose critical. Regardless of the label, the self-directed learner must develop the ability to identify, prioritize, select, validate, evaluate, and interpret information obtained through the processing skills. Information is not equal; some is more useful than others for given purposes. Learners who are unable to establish some kind of observation protocol based on learning goals are unlikely to be self-directed learners. The successful self-directed learner develops the ability to determine and evaluate the sources of information, as well as the reliability, validity, and meaning of information (including theories and other explanations).

6) Self-Awareness

The successful self-directed learner has the ability to be aware of "self." This attribute is closely related to some of the executive processes identified with metacognition. It enables individuals to be aware of their learning processes, to be aware of their weaknesses and strengths, to know if they can call up additional powers of concentration, to know their ability to use a different approach, to know how and what is distracting in their environment, to know the importance of a given learning activity, to know when they need assistance, and to have a realistic perception of their ability to achieve their learning goal.

Source: http://faculty-staff.ou.edu/L/Huey.B.Long-1/Articles/sd/selfdirected.html

Exhibit 4-2: Research on Traits of Self-Directed Learners

Learner Traits	Research*	Classroom Implications
Student Motivation	Anderman, 2004; Guthrie, Alao, & Rinehart, 1997; Howse, Lange, Farran, & Boyles, 2003; Lumsden, 1994, 1999	Challenging, but achievable, relevant assignments; conceptual theme instruction; choice in task/task accomplishment; mastery learning/outcome-based instruction; cooperative/collaborative learning; individual goal setting; accelerated learning; teacher modeling of positive behaviors; depth rather than breadth of topics.
Goal Orientation	Caraway, Tucker, Reinke, & Hall, 2003; Nichols, Jones, & Hancock, 2003; Stefanou & Parkes, 2003	Type of assessment influences motivation; learner emotions/teacher instructional strategies influence student goal orientation; a higher general level of confidence increases student engagement in curriculum.
Locus of Control	Harlen & Crick, 2003; Miller, Fitch, & Marshall, 2003	Learning goals rather than performance goals; at-risk students have a higher external locus of control.
Self-Efficacy	Bouffard & Couture, 2003; Linnenbrink & Pintrich, 2003; Thomas, 1993; Zimmerman, 2002	Student demonstrates behavioral, cognitive, motivational engagement; teachers assist students to maintain self-efficacy beliefs; foster belief that competence/ability is changeable; motivational variables do not change much across subject matter; performance feedback improves independent learning.
Self-Regulation	Palmer & Wehmeyer, 2003	Students can develop self-regulation through problem-solving/goal-setting instructional activities.
Metacognition	Blakey & Spence, 1990; Ngeow & Kong, 2001	Students should plan, monitor, and evaluate their thinking processes; students should engage in inquiry/problem-based learning that includes problem framing, data gathering, divergent thinking, idea generation, evaluating alternatives.

*Anderman, L.H. (2004). Student motivation across subject-area domains. *Journal of Educational Research, 97*(6), 283-285; Guthrie, J.T., Alao, S., & Rinehart, J.M. (1997). Engagement in reading for young adolescents. *Journal of Adolescent and Adult Literacy, 40*(6), 438-446; Howse, R.B., Lange, G., Farran, D.C., & Boyles, C.D. (2003). Motivation and self-regulation as predictors of achievement in economically disadvantaged young children. *Journal of Experimental Education, 71*(2), 151-174; Lumsden, L. (1994). *Student motivation to learn* [ERIC digest No. 92]. Eugene, OR: ERIC Clearinghouse on Educational Management. (ERIC Document Reproduction Service No. ED370200); Lumsden, L. (1999). *Student motivation: Cultivating a love of learning.* Eugene, OR: ERIC Clearinghouse on Educational Management. (ERIC Document Reproduction Service No. ED443135); Caraway, K., Tucker, C.M., Reinke, W.M., & Hall, C. (2003). Self-efficacy, goal orientation, and fear of failure as predictors of school engagement in high school students. *Psychology in the Schools, 40*(4), 417-427; Nichols, W.D., Jones, J.P., & Hancock, D.R. (2003). Teachers' influence on goal orientation: Exploring the relationship between eighth graders' goal orientation, their emotional development, their perceptions of learning, and their teachers' instructional strategies. *Reading Psychology, 24*(1), 57-85; Stefanou, C., & Parkes, J. (2003). Effects of classroom assessment on student motivation in fifth-grade science. *Journal of Educational Research, 96*(3), 152-162; Harlen, W., & Crick, R.D. (2003). Testing and motivation for learning. *Assessment in Education, 10*(2), 169-207. Retrieved December 7, 2004, from www.educationarena.com/educationarena/sample/sample_pdfs6/CAIE10_2.pdf ; Miller, C.A., Fitch, T., & Marshall, J.L. (2003). Locus of control and at-risk youth: A comparison of regular education high school students and students in alternative schools. *Education, 123*(3), 548-552; Bouffard, T., & Couture, N. (2003). Motivational profile and academic achievement among students enrolled in different school tracks. *Educational Studies, 29*(1), 19-38; Linnenbrink, E.A., & Pintrich, P.R. (2003). The role of self-efficacy in student engagement and learning in the classroom. *Reading and Writing Quarterly: Overcoming Learning Difficulties, 19*(2), 119-137; Thomas, J.W. (1993). Promoting independent learning in the middle grades: The role of instructional support practices. *Elementary School Journal, 93*(5), 575-591; Zimmerman, B.J. (2002). Becoming a self-regulated learner: An overview. *Theory into Practice, 41*(2), 64-70; Palmer, S.B., & Wehmeyer, M.L. (2003). Promoting self-determination in early elementary school: Teaching self-regulated problem-solving and goal-setting skills. *Remedial and Special Education, 24*(2), 115-126; Blakey, E., & Spence, S. (1990). *Developing metacognition* [ERIC digest]. Syracuse, NY: ERIC Clearinghouse on Information Resources. (ERIC Document Reproduction Service No. ED327218); Ngeow, K., & Kong, Y. (2001). *Learning to learn: Preparing teachers and students for problem-based learning* [ERIC digest]. Bloomington, IN: ERIC Clearinghouse on Reading, English, and Communication. (ERIC Document Reproduction Service No. ED457524).

Source: http://www.nwrel.org/planning/reports/self-direct/index.php. Used by permission of Northwest Regional Educational Laboratory, 101 SW Main St., Suite 500, Portland, OR 97204-3213, 1.800.547.6339

Drawing on the situational leadership model popularized by Paul Hersey and Ken Blanchard, Gerald Grow relates the teacher's or trainer's role to the learner's relative readiness and preparation to learn (http://www.longleaf.net/ggrow). This model has intuitive appeal. Learners progress through four stages just as leaders do in the situational leadership model:

- In Stage 1, learners are dependent and need a trainer who serves as an authority, subject matter expert, and coach. Trainers who behave appropriately for the needs of learners in Stage 1 will provide information and give lectures.
- In Stage 2, learners are interested, but need a trainer who serves as motivator and guide. Appropriate actions for trainers include providing guided discussions and goal-setting efforts.
- In Stage 3, learners are involved but need a trainer to serve as facilitator. Trainers should guide learners in projects.
- And finally, in Stage 4, learners are fully self-directed. They need a trainer who serves as a learning coach. They can pursue self-directed learning projects, and the trainer is a resource and an enabling agent to help learners locate appropriate people, places, and resources to support their learning.

Free agent learners lack a single, agreed-upon definition, just as self-directed learners do. Free agent athletes are those who are free of contractual responsibilities and can negotiate with other teams. Similarly, free agent learners can be seen as highly independent learners who do not demonstrate loyalty to any one source of information or training—or to any group. As mentioned in chapter 3, free agent learners are "self-directed learners on steroids" (Rothwell, 2002). They are driven to get usable results quickly to help them cope with their problems. Their model for learning is often to rely on search engines to source information of value to them. They know how to skim and filter vast sources of information rapidly to find something to meet their immediate learning needs.

An alternative but not contradictory way to understand free agent learners is that they are completely self-oriented—they are "out for themselves." Showing little or no loyalty to one employer, they are determined to make themselves more employable and attractive in the labor market by continually updating their skills. They expect their employers to provide them with sufficient challenge to develop them for the future, whether inside or outside the organization. To them, an employer's willingness to invest in training and professional development is an important factor in attracting and retaining these talented people.

Employers generally want self-directed learners who are willing to take responsibility for their own learning. But satisfying free agent learners is more difficult. They want highly practical training that can be applied immediately. And they want to be sufficiently challenged so that they can remain employable in a highly uncertain labor market in which layoffs and company bankruptcies may throw people out of work without regard to their performance or potential. Free agent learners pride themselves on being ready to jump employers, and even occupations, quickly. Agility in learning is what they prize and what they demonstrate. Trainers can and do find it challenging to deal with such hyperactive, aggressive learners.

Think About This

It may not matter whether learners are self-directed or are free agent learners. Simply assume that all learners want to possess practical knowledge that they can use immediately. If you do that, you will seldom be far off from the realities of today's workplace.

Generational Differences Among Adult Learners

Focusing on generational differences is just one way to think about *learner analysis*, a process of carefully analyzing a group of learners who are to participate in a planned learning experience. Just as audience analysis is essential to public speaking and market analysis is essential to selling a product or service, so learner analysis is essential to designing, developing, and delivering effective instruction. Much has been written about learner analysis, and there are many ways to analyze learners (for instance, Rothwell & Kazanas, 2008, and *Chapter 4: Instructional Analysis: Analyzing the Learners* at http://www.angelfire.com/la2/learners/learners.html).

Still, in recent years, many management authorities have focused attention on differences in generations in terms of their attitudes about work, life, work/life balance, and even learning.

The key groups to consider are Baby Boomers, Generation X, Generation Y, and Generation Z.

Baby Boomers were born between 1946 and 1964. They were a cohort born immediately following World War II, both in the United States and in many other countries that participated in that war. Boomers make up more than 20 percent of the U.S. population. While not all Boomers share the same characteristics, they are generally known to have a demanding work ethic. They have worked hard for what they achieved. They expect other people to be as responsible as they are. They have a sense of urgency, seeking to get results with a no-nonsense approach.

Gen X, sometimes called the *baby bust generation*, was born immediately after the Boomers, generally between 1965 and 1980. The term *Gen X* was popularized by a novel written by Douglas Coupland in 1991. Coupland characterized people born during this time to be cynics. They lack motivation and are frustrated. Their work ethic is not at all like the Boomers, who become upset with the attitude of Gen Xers.

Gen Y—sometimes called *millennials* or (amusingly) *Gen Why?*—was born between 1979 and 1999. They are hardworking people, like the Boomers, and are worried most about jobs, careers, health care, and being able to afford a lifestyle akin to that of the Boomers. They are serious and work oriented. Some accuse them of being "money hungry." Gen Y workers sometimes question the necessity of "going into work" when they can send their work by email from anywhere in the world. They prefer the freedom to do their work wherever they want and whenever they want. They resist old-style "9 to 5" work schedules in old-style office settings. Gen Ys are impatient with typical work arrangements and expect to receive immediate rewards for their contributions. They do not wish to progress through a journeyman period to prove themselves as previous generations have had to do.

Gen Y makes up about 26 percent of the U.S. population and is much larger—by a factor of three—than Gen X. Only one in three is Caucasian, making this generation the most racially and ethnically diverse of any U.S. generation yet. Many—about one in four—live in single-parent households because of high divorce rates. They have about $100 per week in disposable income. They are virtually connected: About 75 to 90 percent have access to a home computer, and about 50 percent have Internet access at home. Their peers have a major influence on their thinking and on their purchases. (For more information, see http://www.library.csuhayward.edu/staff/ginno/ACRL/demograp.htm).

Gen Z, sometimes called the *new silent generation*, was born in 1995 or after. Today they are children, but they will be the leaders and workers of the future. In most developed nations, they were born at a time when mothers delayed their marriages and births. Expected to have the longest life expectancy of any generation due to improvements in health care and understanding of nutrition, they are technologically savvy, enjoy the financial status established by their parents, network through YouTube and My Space and play the Internet-based game Second Life. They tend to expect everything to be on the web—and think of the Internet first when the topic of communication comes up. They have less patience than previous generations because they are accustomed to everything occurring at nano speed.

Think About This

Begin a learning experience by asking the learners to reflect on their generational differences and how that may, or may not, influence their perceptions about the topic and about the learning methods. By doing this, you avoid stereotyping and engage learners on reflecting on this issue among themselves.

Influences of Generational Differences on Adult Learner Expectations

While it is not a good idea to base learning decisions on stereotypical thinking about differences among generations, it is a good idea to analyze the learners who are targeted for any learning experience. It is best to involve them in the process of deciding what learning is needed, how it is designed and developed, how it is delivered, how transfer of training is planned and embedded in the learning experience, and how results are evaluated.

Still, are there general ideas or tips that can be obtained by examining the general characteristics of the various generations? Here are some suggestions—which will need to be checked against the individuals within any targeted group of learners—for designing and delivering learning experiences for these generations:

Baby Boomers

- Tell them why they should personally care about a learning experience. (Explain what's in it for them.)
- Point out to them how the organization will gain by them changing how they perform or applying what they learn.
- Be aware of their sense of urgency, and be sure to manage time effectively in any learning event.
- Take advantage of their extensive experience, posing them with opportunities to share what they have learned and transfer knowledge they have acquired from experience.

Gen X

- Play down their cynicism, and show them how applying what they learn can benefit other people, as well as themselves.
- When they challenge the training content and process—which they may do—avoid becoming defensive, and ask other participants in the training what they think.
- Invite them to participate in the discussion to give them a way to "vent."
- Challenge other groups to respond to the points made by this group.

Gen Y

- Involve this group in training and otherwise pay attention to them, because they are the most likely of any group to leave the organization.
- Show how training can help them meet their personal and organizational goals, ambitious though they may be.
- Realize that, like previous generations, they often feel defined by their work and are therefore quite eager to improve what they do and what results they obtain.
- Be aware that members of this group are heavily influenced by the opinions of their peers, and therefore make a deliberate effort to appeal to group opinion leaders when designing and delivering learning experiences.
- Use technology with this group, since they like the speed associated with being "linked in."

Gen Z is not yet in the workforce. However, they will pose a challenge in the future in that they will probably expect problems to be solved at nano speed. They may have trouble concentrating, because they are used to skimming much information and only zeroing in on what meets their needs at the moment.

Getting It Done

Chapter 4 explored the differences between self-directed and free agent learners. The chapter also explored the generational differences and how these differences affect adult learning. Here are some key points, along with some suggestions to help you apply what you have learned.

Most learners are self-directed and can be trained to be more self-directed. Review the traits of strong self-directed learners (Exhibit 4-1). Think about how you might use this list to develop the self-directed learning skills of your learner population, including the following:

1. Goal-setting skills

____

____

2. Information-processing skills

____

____

3. Cognitive skills

____

____

4. Content knowledge (competence)

____

____

5. Decision-making skills

___

___

6. Self-awareness

___

___

The chapter also discussed free agent learners and the differences between self-directed and free agent learners. Review this section of the chapter and the descriptions provided of the Baby Boomers and Generations X, Y, and Z. While the chapter provided pointers on effective learning strategies for these groups of learners, you can certainly expand the list. Pose the following questions (and others you might develop from reading this chapter) to members of different generations in your organization. Do they agree or disagree with these concepts? How might you incorporate their answers into the way your own learning events are designed, delivered, and evaluated in your organization?

1. Why do you want to learn? What's your motivation for developing new skills, knowledge, or abilities?

___

___

2. How do you like to learn? Do you learn best in the classroom or online? What kind of participation in learning is important to you?

___

___

3. Where do you like to learn? Do you learn best when other people are around or on your own?

___

___

5

Managing Cultural Differences in Learners

What's Inside This Chapter

In this chapter, you'll learn:

- What *cultural intelligence* is
- How cultural intelligence influences adult learning
- How language is important in training adults of different cultures, and how language issues should be addressed
- What the nature of different national cultures is
- How national cultures affect effective adult learning practices.

What Is *Cultural Intelligence*?

Cultural intelligence (CQ) was a term coined by Christopher Earley and Elaine Mosakowski in a *Harvard Business Review* article published in 2004. According to them, CQ is an ability to deal with national, corporate, and occupational cultures. *Culture*, of course, refers to unspoken beliefs about the right and wrong ways to behave.

Sharing certain features of emotional intelligence (EQ), CQ has to do with distinguishing culturally grounded behaviors from those that are idiosyncratic (individual) or norm based (unique to a group). There are three sources of CQ, according to Earley and Mosakowski: head, body, and heart. The head has to do with the cognitive and rote learning about faux pas in order to understand and avoid violating basic cultural expectations. (A simple example would be understanding that males do not shake hands with some Muslim women, since it is not culturally accepted.) The body has to do with demonstrating awareness of cultural norms and expectations, thereby "winning over" foreign people. (An example might be showing awareness that traditional Chinese women are sometimes reluctant to talk when higher-status, especially male, individuals are present.) The heart centers around motivational and emotional aspects of culture.

CQ is growing more important for business people and for trainers alike. As globalization has become part of the modern world, successful business people and trainers must know how to relate to other cultures. It is important to avoid common gaffes and also demonstrate sensitivity to cultural norms.

How Cultural Intelligence Influences Adult Learning

The first step in mastering cultural intelligence is being open to learning about other cultures. If trainers are unclear whether an approach will work, they should ask. For this reason, it is often wise to prepare instruction early and then ask some cultural informants—people familiar with both the target culture and the initiating culture—to review it. If trainers are from the United States, for instance, they should seek out several—not just one—informants from the target culture and invite them to review training content and approaches to see if they will work in the targeted culture. This simple form of formative evaluation is often essential to ensure the effectiveness of training cross-culturally. Of course, live rehearsals are even better, if time permits.

Managing Language Issues

Language is the embodiment of culture. A national culture is embedded in its language and its mythology. Understanding the languages of other cultures is important in gaining a deeper understanding of those cultures.

However, in today's business world, it is rare that trainers have time to master all the languages they may be called on to use. In one real-world situation, a trainer was tasked to roll out an online training program in 11 nations in 15 different languages within six months! If that is the environment in which trainers must function, they have little time to learn all the languages.

At the same time, if training is to be conducted in native languages rather than in English, it is important to distinguish between translating words and translating concepts. To translate words, a bilingual trainer may translate a training program from English into another language. Then another bilingual trainer, who has not seen the English version, is asked to translate the training program from the foreign language back into English. By checking the two English versions, the trainers may double-check the quality of the translation and make corrections accordingly.

But concept translation may require additional levels of review. Sometimes it is not easy or even possible to make a concept clearly understood. Explaining entrepreneurship to people who have grown up in a Soviet-style Marxist culture, for instance, may not be a simple matter, since they might reject the underlying assumptions or values implicit in the instruction. Still, using cultural informants can be helpful to see how well the training translates conceptually.

What Is the Nature of Different National Cultures?

Two Dutch culturalists are perhaps the most famous for their work on cross-cultural issues. One is Geert Hofstede; the other is Fons Trompenaars. They classified national cultures according to different dimensions. While there is no substitute for going to the authors' original works, it is worth summarizing that work here and then explaining how it may affect adult learning practice.

While at IBM between 1967 and 1973, Hofstede conducted a research study that involved collecting data from more than 100,000 people from 40 countries. From that research study, he initially classified national cultures according to four key dimensions:

- **Power Distance:** This dimension centers on the degree to which members of a society accept the unequal distribution of power in institutions and organizations.

- **Uncertainty Avoidance:** This refers to how much members of a society experience discomfort with uncertainty.
- **Individualism:** This dimension focuses on the degree to which individuals are expected to care for themselves. It stands in stark contrast to collectivism, in which individuals are positioned within a closely knit social network consisting of family, friends, and colleagues.
- **Masculinity:** This refers to how much individuals focus attention on achievement, assertiveness, and consumer-oriented materialism. Masculinity stands in stark contrast to femininity, cultures in which preferences are shown for relationships, balanced work and life, and family.

Of course, stereotypes are dangerous. Not all individuals in any culture match all the generalizations about that nation's culture. But distinguishing cultures provides people with a means to talk about this complex topic. Awareness of culture provides business people—and trainers—with clues about how people relate to each other in different nations. One way to understand the relationship between power distance and uncertainty avoidance in different national cultures is shown in Exhibit 5-1.

Trompenaars focuses more recently on discussing culture as it influences individuals. Just as Hofstede is critical of Trompenaars, so too is Trompenaars critical

Exhibit 5-1: Interaction of National Value Systems and Organizational Forms

		Uncertainty Avoidance	
		Low	**High**
Power Distance	**Low**	Village market, Adhocracy (England, Anglo, Nordic)	Well-oiled machine, Impersonal (Germany, Central Europe)
	High	Family (India, Asia, Africa)	Pyramid, Bureaucracy (France, Latin, Mediterranean)

Source: http://www-rcf.usc.edu/~fulk/Hofstede.html. Used by permission.

of Hofstede. In Charles Hampden-Turner and Fons Trompenaars' book *Riding the Waves of Culture: Understanding Diversity in Global Business* (1997), they discuss culture according to the following dimensions (based on the summary found at http://changingminds.org/explanations/culture/trompenaars_culture.htm):

- **Universalism versus particularism:** Universalism focuses on finding rules; particularism focuses on finding exceptions or special cases.
- **Analyzing versus integrating:** Analysis examines details; integrating examines the big picture.
- **Individualism versus communitarianism:** Individualism centers on individual rights; communitarianism centers on rights of the group, organization, or society.
- **Inner-directed versus outer-directed:** The inner-directed is about individual judgment; outer-directed is about relying on information from the outside world.
- **Time as sequence versus time as synchronization:** Time as sequence views time sequentially; time as synchronization views time in tandem or in parallel.
- **Achieved status versus ascribed status:** Individuals who have achieved status have acquired it through their own performance; individuals who have ascribed status gain it by seniority or by birthright. Achieved status assumes individuals and organizations earn and lose their status every day and that other approaches are recipes for failure.
- **Equality versus hierarchy:** Equality is about the assumption that all people are of equal status; hierarchy recognizes differences among people, with some given higher rank than others.

All of the factors identified by Hofstede and by Trompenaars provide a foundation for thinking about and planning for cultural differences and similarities.

How National Cultures Affect Effective Adult Learning Practices

Despite many years of attention devoted to the important ways that globalization, diversity, and culture should influence learning practices, surprisingly little research and practice have been devoted to trying to incorporate these factors. Many learning experiences still occur in group settings, whether online or in a classroom, with an implicit one-size-fits-all approach. Little effort is made to customize learning experiences to unique cultural conditions.

But Hofstede has provided guidance to educators and trainers alike on what they should do to adapt learning experiences to cultural conditions. He provides this advice in detail in "Cultural Differences in Teaching and Learning," published in the *International Journal of Intercultural Relations* (1986) and in his book *Culture and Organizations* (1991). Hofstede frames his advice for facilitators by the different types of cultures. It is presented in Exhibit 5-2.

Examine Hofstede's tips and reflect on what they might mean for training in your organization. What principles do you agree with? Disagree with? Why?

According to Guild and Garger (1998), educators and trainers should not assume that everyone learns the same way in all cultures. To begin planning for adapting learning experiences to different cultural contexts, educators and trainers should pose a series of questions:

- What outcomes should be expected for all participants?
- What experiences should every participant have?
- What instructional plans should be uniform and standardized?
- How can trainers work toward a common mission while honoring diversity and cultural differences?

These questions—along with the practical tips provided by Hofstede—can offer a starting point for trainers to consider how to align learning with national culture.

Andy Gillett also offers excellent and practical cross-cultural advice for instructors (see http://www.uefap.com/articles/arena.htm). He suggests that trainers working cross-culturally should focus attention on five key issues: (1) cultural behavior, (2) participants' perceptions and expectations, (3) culture, (4) cross-cultural pragmatics, and (5) language.

Cultural behavior involves being aware of how people in different cultural settings use "silence, time, distance and personal space, touching, body language, posture and movement, and eye contact." *Participants' perceptions and expectations* centers on what is expected of instructors, learners, and the learning process. What are the norms of education in a culture? For instance, how often are participants expected to pose questions compared to relying entirely on the teacher. *Culture* has

Exhibit 5-2: Hofstede's Advice for Adult Educators and Trainers in Different Cultures

Small Power Distance Societies	Large Power Distance Societies
1 Stress on impersonal "truth," which can in principle be obtained from any competent person	2 Stress on personal "wisdom," which is transferred in the relationship with a particular teacher (guru)
3 A teacher should respect the independence of his/her students	4 A teacher merits the respect of his/her students
5 Student-centered education (premium on initiative)	6 Teacher-centered education (premium on order)
7 Teacher expects students to initiate communication	8 Students expect teacher to initiate communication
9 Teacher expects students to find their own paths	10 Students expect teacher to outline paths to follow
11 Students may speak up in spontaneously in class	12 Students speak up in class only when invited by the teacher
13 Students allowed to contradict or criticize teacher	14 Teacher is never contradicted nor publicly criticized
15 Effectiveness of learning related to amount of two-way communication in class	16 Effectiveness of learning related to excellence of the teacher
17 Outside class, teachers are treated as equals	18 Respect for teachers is also shown outside class
19 In teacher/student conflicts, parents are expected to side with the student	20 In teacher/student conflicts, parents are expected to side with the teacher
21 Younger teachers are more liked than older teachers	22 Older teachers are more respected than younger teachers
Collectivist Societies	**Individualist Societies**
23 Positive association in society with whatever is rooted in tradition	24 Positive association in society with whatever is "new"
25 The young should learn; adults cannot accept student role	26 One is never too old to learn: "permanent education"
27 Students expect to learn how to do	28 Students expect to learn how to learn
29 Individual students will only speak up in class when called upon personally by the teacher	30 Individual students will speak up in class in response to a general invitation by the teacher
31 Individuals will only speak up in small groups	32 Individuals will speak up in large groups
33 Large classes split socially into smaller cohesive subgroups based on particularist criteria (e.g., ethnic affiliation)	34 Subgroupings in class vary from one situation to the next based on universalist criteria (e.g., the task "at hand")
35 Formal harmony in learning situations should be maintained at all times (T-groups are taboo)	36 Confrontation in learning situations can be salutary; conflicts can be brought into the open
37 Neither the teacher nor any student should ever be made to lose face	38 Face-consciousness is weak

(continued on next page)

Exhibit 5-2: Hofstede's Advice for Adult Educators and Trainers in Different Cultures (continued)

Collectivist Societies (continued)	Individualist Societies (continued)
39 Education is a way of gaining prestige in one's social environment and of joining a higher status group	40 Education is a way of improving one's economic worth and self-respect based on ability and competence
41 Diploma certificates are important and displayed on walls	42 Diploma certificates have little symbolic value
43 Acquiring certificates, even through illegal means (cheating, corruption), is more important than acquiring competence	44 Acquiring competence is more important than acquiring certificates
45 Teachers are expected to give preferential treatment to some students (e.g., based on ethnic affiliation or on recommendation by an influential person)	46 Teachers are expected to be strictly impartial
Feminine Societies	**Masculine Societies**
47 Teachers avoid openly praising students	48 Teachers openly praise good students
49 Teachers use average students as the norm	50 Teachers use best students as the norm
51 System rewards students' social adaptation	52 System rewards students' academic performance
53 A student's failure at school is a relatively minor accident	54 A student's failure at school is a severe blow to his/her self-image and may in extreme cases lead to suicide
55 Students admire friendliness in teachers	56 Students admire brilliance in teachers
57 Students practice mutual solidarity	58 Students compete with each other in class
59 Students try to behave modestly	60 Students try to make themselves visible
61 Corporal punishment severely rejected	62 Corporal punishment occasionally considered salutary
63 Students chose academic subjects in view of intrinsic interest	64 Students chose academic subjects in view of career opportunities
65 Male students may choose traditionally feminine academic subjects	66 Male students avoid traditionally feminine academic subjects
Weak Uncertainty Avoidance Societies	**Strong Uncertainty Avoidance Societies**
67 Students feel comfortable in unstructured learning situations: vague objectives, broad assignments, no timetables	68 Students feel comfortable in structured learning situations: precise objectives, detailed assignments, strict timetables
69 Teachers are allowed to say "I don't know"	70 Teachers are expected to have all the answers
71 A good teacher uses plain language	72 A good teacher uses academic language

Weak Uncertainty Avoidance Societies (continued)	Strong Uncertainty Avoidance Societies (continued)
73 Students are rewarded for innovative approaches to problem solving	74 Students are rewarded for accuracy in problem solving
75 Teachers are expected to suppress emotions (and so are students)	76 Teacher are allowed to behave emotionally (and so are students)
77 Teachers interpret intellectual disagreement as a stimulating exercise	78 Teachers interpret intellectual disagreement as personal disloyalty
79 Teachers seek parents' ideas	80 Teachers consider themselves experts who cannot learn anything from lay parents—and parents agree

Source: http://people.bath.ac.uk/edsjcc/Hofstededimensions.htm

to do with assumptions about the degree to which trainers and learners are expected to be aware of each others' culture. *Cross-cultural pragmatics* is concerned with expectations cross-culturally about how much trainers and learners should engage in complimenting, apologizing, making requests, and inviting the learner to do something. Finally, *language* has to do with what assumptions can be made about language skills. To what extent, for instance, do learners understand English (if that is to be the language in which instruction is to be conducted)? Will they be able to understand the English of others from their own culture? Should a translator be used, and (if so) what kind (simultaneous or sequential)?

Getting It Done

In chapter 5, you learned about cultural intelligence and how it does—or should—influence adult learning. You also learned how language is important in training adults of different cultures and how language issues should be addressed. Care should be taken to make assumptions about adult learning cross-culturally. Ideas that might work in Western cultures may not always work in other cultures. As a means of applying what you learned in this chapter, try to find an individual from outside the United States and interview him or her about what approaches work especially well—or not so well—in his or her home culture. Compare and contrast what you hear to what is presented in this chapter.

1. How might cultural intelligence affect how a training needs assessment is conducted? Note some ideas in the space below:

____

____

____

2. How might cultural intelligence affect how a training program is designed and developed?

____

____

____

3. How might cultural intelligence affect how a training program is delivered?

____

____

____

4. How might cultural intelligence affect how a training program is evaluated?

____

____

____

6

Making Learning Environment a Key to Success

What's Inside This Chapter

In this chapter, you'll learn:

- What *learning climate* is
- What the *learning organization* is
- What *organizational learning* is
- What *small group learning* is
- What the relationship is among adult learning and learning climate, the learning organization, organizational learning, and small group learning
- How the learning climate influences adult learning
- How the learning climate is improved.

What Is *Learning Climate?*

Learning climate is the psychological "feel" about learning in the organization. A fundamental principle of adult learning is that adults must feel psychologically "safe" to learn. Learning can be risky, since mistakes can be made during the learning process. Adults are less willing to "lose face" than younger workers. They are thus generally more emotionally invested in how they perform in learning situations and in how others perceive them when they make mistakes. For this reason, learning climate is critical to the success of adult learning in workplace settings.

Learning climate has to do with answers to questions such as, do individual workers feel that they are encouraged or discouraged from

- developing themselves professionally?
- learning in real time to solve work-related problems?
- declaring their career goals and pursuing them, even when they are not aligned with their supervisors' expectations?
- using work time and organizational resources to enhance their knowledge, skills, and attitudes to achieve higher performance and productivity?

Rothwell (2000) conducted research on learning climate, interviewing over 100 people from different industries and nine different levels of the chain of command. He identified numerous factors that can be measured regarding learning climate. (See Exhibit 6-1.)

Learning culture, on the other hand, refers to the taken-for-granted assumptions about learning. Noted culture authority Edgar Schein, now a retired MIT professor, defined corporate culture as the sum total of acquired experience of an organization or group of people. It is the acquired wisdom that results from work experience—successful or unsuccessful. From experience, people learn what they should do, how they should do it, and what to expect from what they do. Assumptions based on that experience form the culture. Learning culture is thus formed by assumptions based on what approaches to learning work best or not so well.

How Does Learning Climate Affect Individual Learning? People will generally do what they believe they will be rewarded for and avoid doing what they believe they will be punished (or simply not rewarded) for doing. The same principle applies to learning climate. If people feel that work-related learning is not encouraged, they will be less likely to engage in it. It seems reasonable to expect that executives,

Exhibit 6-1: Conditions That Encourage Workplace Learning

Workplace learning is encouraged to the extent that each of the following conditions is perceived to be met:

- Sufficient financial resources exist to support workplace learning.
- Realistic goals and expectations for learning have been established.
- The organization has made a commitment to the learning process.
- Sufficient trust exists in the organization.
- Management shares a common understanding of vision and goals.
- Sufficient time is provided to permit learning.
- Good communication exists in the organization.
- The organization fosters a means by which to collect and use feedback from customers.
- Workplace learning is made a priority and is tied to performance expectations.
- The leadership of the organization is perceived to support workplace learning.
- Clear milestones have been established for the workplace learning process.
- Managers, union leaders, and learners exhibit buy-in and commitment to learning.
- Individuals are matched to learning experiences for which they have the appropriate education and background.
- The learning effort is closely tied to business needs.
- Work standards are consistently applied within the organization.
- The organization possesses clear methods by which to examine and measure work performance.
- Learners are open-minded and possess an attitude that favors learning.
- Measurement and accountability have been established and linked to the workplace learning process.
- The workplace learning process is guided by a plan.
- A clear sense exists about "next steps" following the workplace learning process.
- The organization's union, if the organization is unionized, supports the workplace learning process/effort.
- External environmental factors support the workplace learning process.
- Fear has been reduced within the organization so that individuals are not afraid to take risks and learn.
- Learners feel empowered.
- Learners feel they have incentives and rewards sufficient to encourage them to pursue workplace learning and see "what's in it for them."
- Responsibilities for who should do what in the workplace learning process have been clarified.

Source: Rothwell, W.J. (2000). *Models for the Workplace Learner.* Unpublished research report.

managers, and supervisors should set out to build and sustain a learning climate that supports learning to solve practical work-related problems or seize work-related competitive opportunities.

Unfortunately, there is sometimes a difference of opinion among workers and managers about just how supportive the learning climate is. One way to find out is to ask workers and managers separately and then compare what they said. Trainers can talk to them individually or in focus groups and ask questions such as the following:

- How much do you feel that this organization encourages people to learn to solve work-related problems?
- How much do you feel that people are given sufficient time, money, and resources to learn?
- What learning experiences are most effective in achieving higher productivity in this organization, and how supportive are managers of providing the necessary time, money, and resources for workers to participate in these learning experiences?

What Are Learning Styles? A *learning style* is an individual's preferred mode or modes of learning. Adults vary from children in how they wish to learn, and individual adults also vary from their peers in how they learn best. While children are usually focused on mastery of content (the *what* or the *subject*), adults are more often focused on process (the *how* or the *learning approach*). Learning style can thus be summarized as the way an individual characteristically responds to, and processes, learning events as they are experienced.

Many learning style assessments have been published to help learners or their facilitators find out how individuals learn best. Some are available for free on the web (for instance, http://www.engr.ncsu.edu/learningstyles/ilsweb.html, http://agelesslearner.com/assess/learningstyle.html, and http://www.aselfportraitonline.net/store/default.asp?promo=L4L100).

Particularly well-known among trainers is the learning style model created by David Kolb (1984). For Kolb, individual learning styles should shape what trainers do by way of instructional approaches. An effective learning culture would accommodate individuals with different learning styles. Kolb's approach focuses heavily on how people process information.

Think About This

How often do trainers really try to accommodate individual learning styles? Look for some training programs offered by your organization or by others, and see how often any effort is explicitly made to tailor the training to individual learning styles. If you do not find many that are, why do you think that is so? What could be done differently so that individual styles are explicitly considered and addressed?

Kolb divided people into four categories. Each category represented a distinctive approach or style for learning:

- *Convergers:* Learners with this style acquire knowledge by analyzing and then applying new concepts. They remain emotionally detached and organize information by deductive reasoning.
- *Divergers:* Learners with this style acquire knowledge by intuition. They grasp the big picture and tend to be very creative. Imagination is the great strength of a diverger.
- *Assimilators:* Learners with this style have the ability to come up with theoretical models. They do not focus on practical application, but focus on developing theories.
- *Accommodators:* Learners with this style rely on intuition and trial-and-error approaches. They ask other people for information. They get things done.

A visual depiction of Kolb's model is shown in Exhibit 6-2.

Mary Endorf and Marie McNeff (1991) devised their own adult learning styles model. They placed their emphasis on learners' emotional and sociological attributes, recognizing five types:

Confident

- Practical
- Self-directed
- Results-oriented
- Can identify and meet his or her own learning needs

Exhibit 6-2: A Visual Depiction of Kolb's Learning Styles

Kolb's Experiential Learning Style

Concrete and Experience (sensing/feeling)

concrete active (activists)

concrete reflective (reflectors)

Test Hypotheses and New Situation (doing/planning)

Reflection and Observation (reviewing/watching)

abstract active (pragmatists)

abstract reflective (theorists)

Abstraction and Generalization (thinking/concluding)

Source: http://www.nwlink.com/~donclark/hrd/history/kolb.html. Used by permission.

- Competes with himself or herself only
- Encourages people to interact and participate
- Always makes meeting personal goals a high priority.

Affective

- Favors feelings in learning
- Avoids conflict with the instructor
- Regards education as an end in it itself.

Learner in Transition

- Develops independence in thought as the top priority
- Has difficulty establishing personal learning goals

- Prefers interactive learning and discussion
- Rejects the notion of receiving information like a "sponge".

Integrated

- Focuses on personal success
- Wants highly participative learning processes
- Wants to be regarded as a meaningful contributor.

Risk Taker

- Feels excitement with new projects
- Enjoys that feeling
- Remains self-confident.

Other researchers have proposed alternative learning style models—such as whether individual learners tend to rely most heavily on the sense of sight, hearing, taste, smell, or touch.

How Do Learning Styles Affect Individual Learning? Learning styles should affect individual learning by influencing how information is presented to learners. Individuals should assess their own learning styles—either by using instruments or simply reflecting on how they learn best. Trainers should consider learning styles when designing and delivering training. One size does not fit all: Some people are tactile learners (touch), some are auditory learners (sound), some are visual learners (sight), and some are a combination of such styles. It is best to try to appeal to a range of styles when providing instruction.

What Are Learning Competencies? A *learning competency* is any characteristic that leads to successful or superior learning. Individuals can build their competencies in doing their jobs, and they can also build their competencies in learning how to learn. Learning competence centers on how well people learn. Organizations should focus on building their workers' learning competencies so that they can more effectively keep pace with the dynamic, and arguably increasing, rate of change.

Exploratory research conducted by William J. Rothwell indicated possible learning competencies. (See Exhibit 6-3.) The research study was based on five industry categories and nine levels of the chain of command. Individuals from each level and each industry category were interviewed, and then the results were coded. While the study results have not been validated with a very large group, they do provide an initial starting point for considering learner competencies.

Exhibit 6-3: Workplace Learning Competencies

1. Reading Skill
2. Writing Skill
3. Computation Skill
4. Listening Skill
5. Questioning Skill
6. Speaking Skill
7. Cognitive Skill
8. Individual Skill
9. Resource Skill
10. Interpersonal Skill
11. Informational and Technological Skill
12. Systems Thinking
13. Personal Mastery
14. Mental Modeling
15. Shared Visioning
16. Team-Learning Skill
17. Self-Knowledge
18. Short-Term Memory Skill
19. Long-Term Memory Skill
20. Subject Matter Knowledge
21. Enjoyment of Learning and Work
22. Flexibility
23. Persistence and Confidence
24. Sense of Urgency
26. Giving Respect to Others
27. Work Environment Analytical Skill
28. Sensory Awareness
29. Open-Mindedness
30. Humility
31. Analytical Skill (synthesis)
32. Intuition
33. Information-Sourcing Skill
34. Information-Gathering Skill
35. Information-Organizing Skill
36. Feedback-Solicitation Skill
37. Willingness to Experiment and Gain Experience
38. Internalization Skill
39. Application of New Knowledge Skill
40. Ability to Adapt Knowledge to New Situations or Events
41. Critical Examination of Information Skill
42. Learning How to Learn Skill
43. Self-Directedness Skill

Source: Rothwell, W.J. (2000). *Models for the Workplace Learner.* Unpublished research report. All rights reserved.

How Do Learning Competencies Relate to Job Competencies? *Job competencies* consist of the knowledge, skills, attitudes, and other characteristics that lead to successful or superior job performance. While job descriptions focus on describing the work, job competencies focus on describing the people who do the work or who are among the most productive people who do the work.

Learning competencies are not the same as job competencies. They focus on how people learn how to learn and how individuals can improve their learning skills to tackle work-related challenges. Learning competencies are thus focused on the process of learning, while job competencies are focused on the process of how successful or best-in-class performers get results/productivity.

How Do Learning Competencies Affect Individual Learning? Learning competencies are essential to learning how to learn and improving how one learns how to learn.

Yet schools and training departments continue to focus on teaching people "subjects" rather than equipping individuals with the learning competence they will need to keep their knowledge, skills, and attitudes current as conditions change over a working lifetime that may encompass several half-lives of all human knowledge. Workers of the future will have to be effective in taking initiative to keep their own knowledge, skills, and attitudes current, and that will require them to demonstrate learning competencies.

Many organizations have focused attention on the competencies associated with effective training and how effective trainers achieve results. However, few organizations (if any) have focused on learning competencies. While trainers are certified in the United States through ASTD and other groups, nobody certifies learners. And yet, which is the larger and more important group?

Think About This

Why would it be worth considering how to improve learning competence? What would happen if learners were more efficient and effective in how they learned how to learn?

How Is the Trainer's Role Influenced by Learning Climate, Learning Styles, and Learning Competencies? The trainer's role is clearly influenced by learning climate, learning styles, and learning competencies. What the trainer does—and should do—is influenced by the background or backdrop in which the training occurs (the learning climate), how people learn (learning styles), and how well people have learned how to learn (learning competencies). While no clear guidelines exist on how to use learning climate, learning styles, and learning competencies together to increase the impact of training, it is worth reflecting on how to do so.

Trainers should therefore ask themselves such questions as these (among others):

- How can the learning climate be made most supportive for a learning effort?
- What are the learning styles of the learners?

- How could learning style be measured and used to best effect?
- How much learning competence have the learners demonstrated?
- How could learning competence be built?

What Is a *Learning Organization?*

A learning organization is not the same thing as learning climate. The term *learning organization* was first used in the 1980s to refer to organizations that tried to experiment with new ways of functioning in the fiercely competitive, dynamic environment that has characterized the global business environment since that time. It has to do with establishing a culture in which learning is prized.

What Is *Organizational Learning?*

Organizational learning should not be confused with learning climate or learning organization. Organizations cannot "learn," of course, in the same way that individuals can. (In fact, thinking that is possible is to be guilty of the fallacy of anthropomorphism—giving an inanimate object or entity the characteristics of human beings.) However, organizations can engage in new experiences and store, in institutional memory, the fruits of those experiences in the memories of individual members and in rituals and artifacts. Changing organizational culture really means encouraging organizational learning, since culture is a byproduct of experience. A *ritual* is set of actions with some kind of symbolic meaning. An example of an organizational ritual might be the rite of passage that newcomers must go through. This might include hazing by experienced organizational members. An *artifact* is an object that has meaning. Examples of organizational artifacts may include job descriptions, policies, procedure manuals, and documented work processes, since they embody institutional memory. Culture is embodied in rituals, artifacts, and in the collective institutional memory of workers.

Organizational learning has become a focus of great interest in recent years, just as the learning organization has. A key goal is to leverage organizational learning to achieve improved organizational performance. According to Klaus Beck (1997), two types of organizational change are key to organizational learning. The first, *adaptive learning*, means "changes that have been made in reaction to changed external environmental conditions." The second, *proactive learning*, means "organizational changes that have been made on a more willful basis." Adaptive learning means minor, incremental change. It is brought about in response to changes in a dynamic business environment. Proactive learning, however, is transformational change that is brought about to seize opportunities before external environmental changes occur. It can be dramatic, leading to quantum leaps in thinking and acting relative to the environment. Numerous authors have written about organizational learning, including Argyris and Schön (1978), Cyert and March (1963), Dodgson (1991), Fiol and Lyles (1985), Levinthal and March (1993), Levitt and March (1988), March and Olsen (1975), and Senge (1990).

What, then, is the difference between the learning organization and organizational learning? According to Mark Smith (2001), the difference can be summarized in this way:

> The literature on organizational learning has concentrated on the detached collection and analysis of the processes involved in individual and collective learning inside organizations; whereas the learning organizations' literature has an action orientation and is geared toward using specific diagnostic and evaluative methodological tools, which can help to identify, promote, and evaluate the quality of learning processes inside organizations. We could argue that organizational learning is the "activity and the process by which organizations eventually reach th[e] ideal of a learning organization" (Finger & Brand, 1999: 136).

What Is *Small Group Learning?*

Small group learning has generally been treated separately from learning climate, learning organizations, and organizational learning. *Small group learning* focuses on individuals learning in small groups. This can occur in classroom-based training through experiential learning activities such as case study analysis, role plays, games, simulations, brainstorming activities, and any other break-out session in which a small group of learners collectively works together to achieve a learning goal. It can occur in electronically mediated training, such as online instruction, in which learners participate in small groups online to achieve a goal. For instance, learners may meet in a chat room to work on an activity. Small group learning can also occur in action learning sets in which individuals are matched up to achieve both a work goal and a learning goal. They are intended to learn from each other as they carry out a work-related activity, such as solving a real-world problem (reducing customer complaints, increasing customer satisfaction, identifying and eliminating work process bottlenecks, and so forth). Finally, small group learning can occur in real time on the job as members of a work group "huddle" to solve a problem or establish a goal.

Small groups cannot "learn" any more than organizations can. Groups are not individuals—only individuals can learn. But small groups can influence learning climate. Consider this: How much are co-workers and supervisors supportive or unsupportive of individual and group problem-solving efforts by which people can learn? Small groups can also undertake their own learning activities. For instance, a work team may attack a work problem, and the process of solving the problem leads to learning, as well as achieving a work result. Individuals, and the group, are developed in the process. The small group can also embody institutional memory (How did we solve these problems in the past? On what basis were previous decisions made?) and can influence individuals based on the unique aspects of a microculture. A *microculture* is the unique culture of a small group within an organization. For instance, the HR department has a microculture that can be distinctly different from that of the accounting department, since members have been socialized in different ways and have different occupational backgrounds.

Small group learning also includes *communities of practice*. These are understood to be special, informal networks of individuals who share interest in a common problem, issue, vision, or goal (Wenger, 1998). They may also share a common passion, enthusiasm, sense of purpose, set of goals, and may even pursue a common line of investigation to seek results. It is a means by which a group can pursue a learning project, comparable to what Tough discussed in his seminal work (1971). Communities of practice may exist on or off the job and may focus on work-related or personally related issues. Communities of practice are quite flexible. They may meet online, in person, or in a combination of the two. Adults who pursue learning efforts to meet their own social needs will find communities of practice an effective venue by which to meet their learning needs and social needs at the same time.

Relating Learning Climate, Learning Organization, Organizational Learning, and Small Group Learning to Adult Learning Practice

Adult learners, as individuals, do not learn in a vacuum; rather, they learn within a larger context. That context greatly influences how willing people are to learn and how willing they are to apply what they learn back in workplace settings. Transfer of learning is influenced by multiple contexts, including the external environment, the national culture, the organizational culture, the community, the department, the supervisor, and the work group. It is also influenced by individual issues, such as expectations of rewards for learning, career goals and aspirations, and individual life-cycle stage. The previous chapter emphasized the importance of the national culture as one context. But the organizational culture also influences how people learn. See Exhibit 6-4 for a depiction of the contexts that may influence individual learning.

Learning climate frames how people feel about the relative support for their learning in the organization. When that climate is less than supportive of learning, individuals will not engage in it unless they are forced to do so to achieve work results. If they do pursue learning in an unsupportive environment, they may pay for it themselves, conceal it from their supervisor or employer, and even use sick and vacation time to engage in it. It is thus important for organizational leaders to assess the climate for learning periodically and take steps, when necessary, to improve it. This is especially true if organizational leaders claim that "people are our greatest asset" and emphasize the importance of talent in achieving organizational results.

The potential of talent is only realized when a supportive learning climate encourages people to exercise their talents and realize their potential.

Exhibit 6-4: The Contexts in Which Adult Learning Occurs

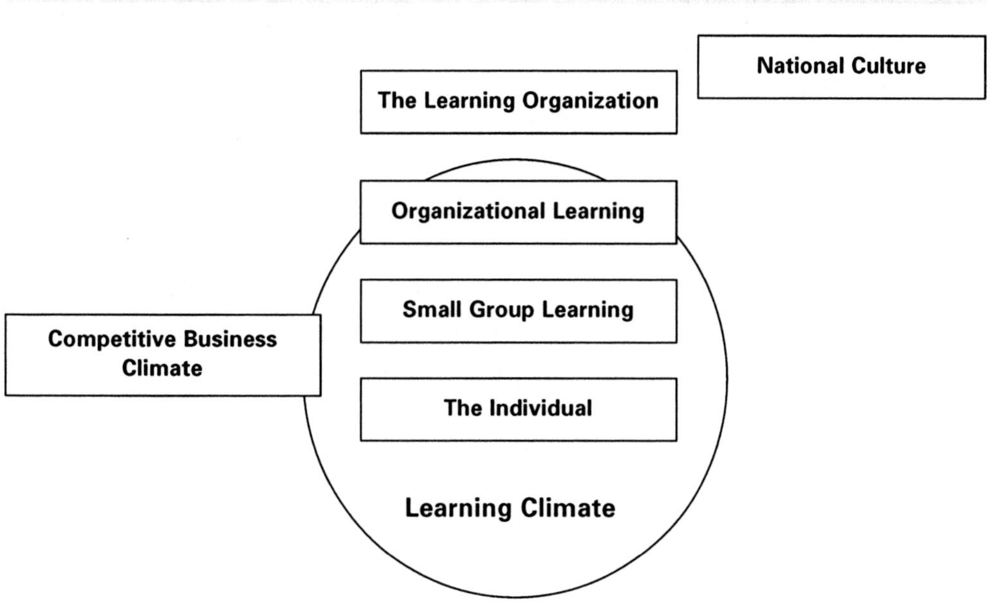

Organizational leaders should pursue the promise of the learning organization. After all, the learning organization is an ideal that can be pursued but may never be fully achieved. They should take steps to pinpoint what business goals or measurable objectives are to be achieved from an effort to build a learning organization, clarify which characteristics are most desirable to be achieved (such as self-mastery, mental models, shared vision, team learning, systems thinking, or others), establish an action plan to implement efforts to cultivate those characteristics in a systematic way, continuously pursue the effort over time, and measure results along the way. By working on realizing the promise of a learning organization, organizational leaders should also be building a learning climate that supports individual learning.

Additionally, organizational leaders should focus attention on organizational learning with the goal in mind of improving organizational performance and productivity. They should identify what rituals, artifacts, and corporate cultural conditions embody organizational learning and work to intensify the identification and transfer of organizational knowledge, skills, and attitudes.

Small group learning is an important means to the end of establishing a supportive learning climate. Most adults have the closest connection to their employer in their *family groups*—that is, their immediate co-workers and supervisor. Consequently, efforts to build learning climate should be geared to establishing and maintaining a supportive learning climate in family groups, as well as in the organization generally.

The learning organization is an important goal for organizational leaders and others in organizations to pursue. By doing so, they will encourage a culture that supports learning. They will also encourage individuals to try new things that may enhance competitive advantage and that they may learn from.

Organizational learning is about enhancing how people carry out the process of learning in groups and then store and pass on that wisdom through rituals, artifacts, and corporate culture. Improving organizational learning will enhance the ability of individuals to learn from their own experience, as well as from others' experiences.

How Learning Climate Influences Adult Learning

How people feel about the learning climate has a major influence on how motivated they are to learn and how willing they are to apply what they learn.

Learning climate consists of more than one place. It includes

- the learning climate of the training setting (such as the classroom setting in which the training is delivered or the online site in which the individual accesses instruction)
- the learning climate of the work setting (such as the work setting in which the individual functions, including his or her immediate supervisor and co-workers)
- the learning climate of the individual (such as the family, spouse, children, and others significant in the individual's life).

If any one of these learning climates is not supportive of individual learning, adults will generally not feel comfortable enough to engage fully in the learning process. The result will be lower-than-expected transfer of training.

How Is Learning Climate Improved?

Action should be taken to improve the learning climate at all three levels—in the training setting, in the work setting, and in the personal setting.

Improving Learning Climate in the Training Setting. Instructors and facilitators should encourage a positive learning climate as quickly as possible, whether in a classroom setting or in an electronically mediated setting. They can do this by encouraging introductions so that people know each other, emphasizing that every question is worthwhile and there is no such thing as a "stupid question," and explaining that all people are expected to participate. Be sure to explain why the training topic is important to the organization and to the participants. Ask learners what they hope to learn and what expectations they may have of the setting—and of each other. If time permits, ask learners to set ground rules for how they will interact and how they will deal with mistakes or misstatements to preserve the dignity of everyone.

Improving Learning Climate in the Work Setting. The learning climate of the work setting is influenced at every stage of the worker's lifecycle. Workers gain early ideas about it from questions and comments made during the selection process; they learn about it in the stories they hear and the gossip that is told by co-workers; they gain experience with it based on comments casually dropped, and formally presented, by their supervisors. Organizational policies and procedures—such as how requests for time to pursue professional development are answered—give individuals a sense of the learning climate.

The supervisor plays a key role in establishing and maintaining a supportive learning climate. If the organization's leaders seek to change learning climate, they must start by focusing attention on supervisors. If organizational leaders truly value learning and professional development, they will establish formal goals—such as key performance indicators—to be achieved by supervisors and their workers at every level of the organization's hierarchy. By doing this, they will establish an accountability system and will also embed consequences for action and nonaction in the system. This will give the organization a new experience, thereby potentially changing corporate culture to be more supportive of learning.

Improving Learning Climate in the Personal Setting. How much do individuals value learning and professional development? How supportive are individuals' family members, friends, or significant others of their efforts to learn and develop? While organizational leaders may not be able to change unsupportive family members or friends directly, they can create incentives that will provide powerful reasons to pursue learning and development. Organizational leaders can also show they care about family opinion by asking about it.

Getting It Done

In chapter 6, you learned how to define *learning climate, learning organization, organizational learning,* and *small group learning.* You also considered what the relationship is among adult learning and learning climate, the learning organization, organizational learning, and small group learning, as well as how learning climate influences adult learning and how learning climate can be improved.

1. How could you assess the learning climate of your organization? Brainstorm some ideas in the space below.

___

___

___

2. How could you improve the learning climate of your organization?

____

____

____

3. If you asked employees about what the organization does to discourage their real-time, on-the-job learning, what might they list as possible obstacles to learning?

____

____

____

7

Putting Technology to Work for Learners

What's Inside This Chapter

In this chapter, you'll learn:

- What the *digital divide* is
- Why the digital divide is important
- What technologies affect adult learning
- How technology affects adult learning, and how technology applications can be improved.

Learning professionals are preoccupied with instructional technology. (*Instructional technology* focuses on how technology can support the learning process.) It is not surprising why. Most of the startling new opportunities in the field have been created by emerging instructional technology. Twenty years ago, for instance, it was unthinkable to envision using iPods, wikipedias, or learning management systems as viable vehicles by which to deliver instruction. While technology advances rapidly, human beings do not. Developments in adult learning theory have been slow in coming, and slower still in fully adapting to applications of technology to enhance adult learning. Nor has organizational management kept pace with the full range of new instructional technologies amid a dizzying, and growing, range of options.

This chapter focuses on the impact of technology on adult learning. While the issue is a complicated one, the intent of this chapter is to review some key issues in how emerging instructional technologies impact adult learning. (For a more robust treatment of this topic, see Rothwell, et al. 2006.)

What Is the *Digital Divide?*

Digital divide refers to differences between people who have access to (or are willing to use) new technology and those who do not (or are not). The assumption is that not all people have equal access to the Internet—or, if they do, they lack the skills or willingness to use it. The digital divide may be most noticeable between men and women, because men initially used the Internet more than women. It may also refer to the difference between urban and rural dwellers, because urban dwellers tend to have easier access to the Internet. The digital divide may refer to the difference between younger and older people, because younger people are often more willing to use the Internet than their parents. Or it may refer to differences between higher- and lower-income groups, because lower-income groups tend to be less willing to use the Internet than higher-income groups. It may even refer to differences between developed and developing economies, because it is easier to gain access to the Internet in developed economies than in developing nations.

Why Is the Digital Divide Important?

To reach adult learners, it is important that they have the skills and the willingness to use new technology. If some people have fewer skills, less access, or are less willing to access new technology than others, this affects how likely it is that specific targeted learner groups can access learning experiences over the web or through alternative instructional media such as iPods, web-based video teleconferencing, audio conferencing, or other media-based learning methods.

The digital divide may also affect to what degree different learner groups are willing to access new technologies. For instance, it is commonly asserted that older people are less willing to use computer-based learning than younger people are.

Consider the following facts and figures about Internet usage (Douglass, 2001—updated 2007):

- The U.S. Internet population grew 25 percent to 164 million in 2001.
- In the second half of 2000, 43 percent of African Americans were online, compared to 34 percent from January to June 2000.
- Latinos also increased their use of the Internet—47 percent of Latinos were online at the end of 2000, compared with 40 percent in the first half of the year.
- Despite increased usage, however, African-American users felt the Internet lacks relevant content for them. Only 37 percent of African Americans felt there was adequate content on the Internet for them, compared with 64 percent of Latinos. Sites specifically providing ethnic content are preferred by 46 percent of African Americans and 38 percent of Latinos.
- Seventy percent of Asian-American households were online, compared with 45 percent to 50 percent of white households.
- American-Indian users logging on at home increased 67 percent, surpassing 800,000 users last year.
- Low-income consumers are accessing the web from home at a faster pace than any other income group; the fastest-growing group of Internet users is factory workers and laborers—9.5 million had home access to the web in March 2001, up from 6.2 million in March 2000.
- Homemakers were the second-fastest-growing group, jumping 49 percent in the past year to 2.5 million.
- Families with lower incomes and less education spend more time online than any other group once they log on; people earning $21,000 to $33,000, typically in blue-collar jobs, spent the most time online in June 2001—11 to 12 hours, compared with the national average of nine hours.
- More than 30 million Internet users belong to the upper middle-class income group (earning between $50,000 to $74,999 a year), making it the largest segment of the online population to access the web from home.
- An almost equal percentage of men and women surf the web now; 50.6 percent of adults with Internet access are women, while 49.4 percent are men. (This represents a shift in usage by gender since the Internet initially became popular.)

- Among rural households, 38.9 percent have Internet access, a 75 percent increase from last year.
- Rural households earning $10,000 or less a year had the lowest personal computer ownership rates (7.9 percent) and online access rates (2.3 percent).
- Only 21.6 percent of people with disabilities are on the Internet, and almost 60 percent have never used a personal computer, compared with 25 percent among the whole population.
- The digital divide is often attributed to race, but income is the predominate factor that determines whether Americans are online.
- Comfort of use and relevancy of content are crucial components to sustained Internet usage by most demographic groups.

The greatest number of Internet users are in Asia, the most populous part of the world (http://www.internetworldstatus.com/stats.htm). But the highest penetration of users in households is in North America.

What Technologies Affect Adult Learning?

It is difficult to list all the new technologies that can be used to assess learning needs, design training and other learning experiences, deliver instruction, and evaluate results.

E-learning, as a term, first entered the popular vernacular in the mid-1990s and, at that time, referred to any instruction lending itself to electronic delivery. E-learning has since divided into two parts: computer-mediated learning and electronically assisted learning. *Computer-mediated learning* encompasses both computer-based training (using personal computers) and online instruction (which includes virtual classrooms). *Electronically assisted learning* encompasses all modes of what is also called *distance learning,* such as video teleconferencing, audio conferencing, electronic whiteboards, videotapes, and many more.

The training community has generally greeted all forms of instructional technology with much excitement. It is regarded as a way to reduce travel costs—often a big-ticket item in organizational training expenses—and increase the size of the audience that can participate in planned learning events. Many managers like instructional technology because it can often be accessed during downtime on workers' desktops, thereby eliminating the need for workers to attend off-the-job training and have their work pile up while away.

However, most trainers today realize that there are limitations to what online or electronically mediated methods can offer. There is a need for creative strategies to design and develop blended learning, which mixes one or many media (including print, audio, video, face-to-face, and many others) to support training delivery (Rothwell et al., 2006).

How Technology Affects Adult Learning

While various media models have been proposed to indicate ways to balance the cost-effectiveness of training delivery with learning effectiveness, there does not seem to be definitive evidence to support how and when to choose different media or how to blend them effectively.

It seems that the biggest adult learning issues associated with instructional technology center on retention or completion rates, learner self-directedness, and interactivity. These issues seem to be related to each other. Learners who are not self-directed need more interactivity if they are to complete online training or other electronically assisted or mediated learning.

Retention or Completion Rates. Some authorities claim that retaining—that is, maintaining enrollment of—learners in technology-mediated instruction is more difficult than in face-to-face experiences. There is thus concern about completion rates for programs and even for individual lessons.

A 2003 survey of university programs revealed that "66 percent of the distance-learning institutions have an 80 percent or better completion rate for their distance education courses, and 87 percent have 70 percent or better completion rates" (Howell, Williams, & Lindsay, 2003).

Yet concerns remain high about retention and completion rates. One question worth asking is this: What steps do these organizations take to include learners beyond online experiences so that they develop a social network of other learners? If the answer is "none," that may be one reason why retention rates are low. People must feel that they have established personal relationships in order to believe that they are part of something bigger than themselves. Without that, alienation can set in—and people will quit online experiences when their social needs are left unmet.

The same problem affects trainers and faculty. If they have few interpersonal interactions face-to-face and merely interact with people online or through other electronically mediated methods, then they too begin to feel alienated—and may become trainer turnover statistics.

Learner Self-Directedness. One consequence of increased reliance on technology is that learners are expected to take more initiative, be more self-directed than in the past. There is no trainer or facilitator in many—even most—online training programs. Learners must proceed through the learning experience at their own pace, motivating themselves. Those accustomed to trainer-led or instructor-led face-to-face delivery methods (like schools) are sorely disappointed by electronic-based learning experiences in which they must take the active role. Learners must not only learn how to learn, but must learn how to motivate themselves to persist. That may be one reason why some learners choose not to finish, particularly learners who pursue learning for social interactions that do not occur when the training is entirely self-directed.

Interactivity. It has become a truism to state that e-learning should be interactive. As Helen Geiger writes, "in the world of e-learning, *interactivity* is any strategy or element used to help the learner process learning. It is accepted truth that *interactivity* is the magic element that makes e-learning both engaging and effective" (Geiger, 2007). The stereotype of an e-learning course that is not interactive is one with a large number of PowerPoint slides posted online. Another example is posting hours of unedited classroom videos on the web for learners to watch. In both cases, such e-learning lacks interactivity or fails to offer learners the chance to participate in the learning process.

Of course, it is not just e-learning that can lack interactivity; classrooms can, too. In some Asian cultures even today, students are forced to listen to hours of lecture. They are publicly ridiculed if they ask questions. Their professors will tell them that "all questions were answered if you were listening closely enough." Not surprisingly, students do not know how to apply what they have learned and often nap through the long, boring recitations without the possibility of even breaking it up by asking questions.

What is the alternative?

Interactivity means engaging, involving, and empowering learners by giving them an active role to play in dealing with content and in the learning process. An often misunderstood term, interactivity does not mean counting how long learners view a webpage, how many webpages they progress through in a specific time period, or even how many tests they take and what scores they receive. Instead, it means how much action the learner must engage in and how much involvement the learner must demonstrate to continue participation in the learning effort. Generally, the more the better.

Hank Kelly distinguishes between learner interactivity with content and learner interpersonal interactivity (http://www.studyoverseas.com/distance/interactivity.htm). *Interactivity with content* gives learners the chance to self-pace and self-control the speed at which they progress through training. Designing such programs can be expensive and time-consuming. But *interpersonal interactivity* encourages learners to develop higher-order critical thinking. They are challenged to think, interact with others online or on site, debate key ideas, create new things, and much more. Just as active training encourages trainers to get the learners active, so interpersonal interactivity in online learning means that learners must become interpersonally engaged in as many ways as possible, as often as possible. In this way, their chance of staying in the training increases, as does the likelihood that they will remember what they learned.

Here are specific tips on increasing interpersonal interactivity in electronically mediated learning:

- Send learners emails.
- Ask learners to participate in online, real-time computer conferences.
- Use instant messenger technology to chat in real time.
- Post questions and ask learners to answer them.
- Require learners to participate in conference calls at specific times.
- Find ways to use video-based learning—or even web-based video, if possible.

Experienced facilitators can undoubtedly think of other ways to engage learners in real time or close to real time.

The challenge for adult educators and trainers in the future will be to familiarize themselves—and the learners they serve—with emerging technologies to support

Basic Rule 6

Any instruction that relies on technology as a major component of delivery should include consideration of retention, learner self-directedness, and interactivity.

instruction. One reason to do that is time savings. Information can be made available via technology in almost real time. But classroom-based training and group learning events should take advantage of their well-documented ability to encourage creative thinking and innovation. In short, in the future, it is quite likely that blended learning will increasingly be used to communicate information, but face-to-face learning events, far from disappearing, will shift to knowledge creation.

Getting It Done

In chapter 7, you learned what the *digital divide* is and why the digital divide is important. You also learned what technologies affect adult learning, how technology affects adult learning, and how technology applications can be improved.

1. What impact might the digital divide have on learning in your organization?

____

____

____

2. What could be done to reduce the impact of the digital divide on your organization? For example, offer training on how to use the computer or create a learning center on using the computer. List other ways below.

____

____

____

3. What issues or challenges might be faced in your organization if you began offering training via a technology that has not been used before? List the challenges and what might be done to overcome those barriers.

____

____

____

8

Using Proven Facilitation Techniques to Drive Learning

What's Inside This Chapter

In this chapter, you'll learn:

- What a *facilitator* is and how a facilitator is different from an *instructor*
- What facilitators should do to clarify roles and set ground rules with groups
- What learners should do in facilitated learning and how the unique characteristics of today's adult learners pose special challenges to facilitators
- What competencies and behaviors are associated with facilitation
- How facilitator behaviors differ, depending on whether learning is delivered on site, online, or in a blended format
- What can be done to improve facilitation skills.

What Is a *Facilitator*, and How Is a Facilitator Different From an *Instructor?*

The word *facilitation* comes from the Latin word *facile*, which means "to make easy." A facilitator's job is to make it easy for group members to work together to surface challenges or opportunities and reach some level of agreement about the nature of the challenge, the causes of the challenge, the solutions appropriate to meet the challenge, the action plans to implement solutions, and the appropriate ways to evaluate results.

In most cases, a facilitator focuses on group dynamics or group process—that is, what is happening in the group—rather than focusing on content or solutions. For that reason, a facilitator often uses questions to help members of a group discuss their issues, articulate their concerns, and reach group agreement on problem causes, problem solutions, action plans for solutions, and evaluation methods.

Instructors, in contrast, are typically expected to be subject matter experts (SMEs). They are supposed to "know their stuff." They gain credibility with an audience by having credentials—such as work experience, advanced degrees, publications, presentations, and consulting experience—that will impress those they work with. As an example, a professor of accounting is expected to have a Ph.D. degree, and often the CPA designation, to establish necessary subject matter credibility to serve as an accounting instructor.

Stated in simple terms, instructors "tell" learners what they should know based on their authority as subject matter experts, whereas facilitators "ask" learners what they think, believing that wisdom and expertise already exists within the group. Instructors must therefore know their subjects; facilitators must know how to work with groups, achieving as much involvement and engagement as possible.

But great care must be exercised when enacting the facilitator's role. Any good idea can be abused—the same is true of facilitation. In fact, the word *facipulation* has been coined to describe the combination of "facilitation" and "manipulation." If managers pretend to facilitate ideas from their workers but have already determined what decision will be made, they are demonstrating facipulation. Consequently, it is important to emphasize that, in a truly facilitated event, no decisions have already been made until ideas are surfaced from a group, and group members agree on some level—either by majority or by consensus—that the decision is worth acting on.

The Role of Facilitators in Clarifying Roles and Ground Rules

A facilitated event is only as good as the combination of the facilitator and the group with which he or she works. For this reason, it is important at the outset of a facilitated event to clarify what is expected of participants. That sometimes takes the form of a facilitated discussion about ground rules for the group or rules of engagement for the group. The keyword here is *collaboration*, meaning a highly involved and interactive group.

As part of this process, facilitators clarify that they are not playing the role of subject matter experts. While there are many ways to get that point across, a typical approach might be to say something like this: "We have all been in school. From that experience, we have often learned to expect that the person at the front of the room is the expert who has all the right answers. But in this event, you are expert, and I am only the helper to ensure that we all work together to surface ideas, pinpoint root causes, find solutions, and come up with action plans and metrics to measure success. In short, you—as a group—are playing the expert role."

Most facilitators, when working with a group, will usually clarify their own roles and expectations for group members first. In setting the initial tone for the group, facilitators must usually make the behavioral expectations clear about what the facilitator will do and what participants should do. In both cases, the value of setting ground rules hinges on demonstrating collaboration while at the same time pulling from the group members their own ground rules for collaboration and interaction.

Of course, coming up with ground rules should typically be a facilitated process. A facilitator might do something like ask a group, "What ground rules should we expect from each other?" The facilitator would then refer to a flipchart in front of the group and pull the ground rules out of the group. As an alternative, a facilitator might also pass out a list of possible ground rules (see Exhibit 8-1), then ask participants what additional rules should be established. The handout will serve as a performance cue, or example, of what kind of rules group members should offer for listing on the flipchart.

When facilitating a group session, good facilitators will usually

- have an agenda with start time, end time, and any break times
- list key questions to be addressed in the meeting (to ensure interaction, the fewer the questions, the better)

- make clear if the meeting is to be recorded and—if it is, explain why, and ask if anyone has objections (if they do, do not record)
- post simple ground rules on the agenda, but encourage participants to add others in a first meeting
- ask each member to commit to participate completely—and clarify that this means he or she should talk or ask a question at least once each hour in every meeting
- watch the time and ensure questions are being addressed in a timely manner

Exhibit 8-1: Sample Ground Rules for a Facilitated Group Session

Here are examples of group ground rules. These are not "cast in stone." Indicate how much you agree with these and feel free to add others as appropriate—or as we go along.

During this meeting, participants should

- respect the ideas of other people
- encourage other people to share ideas
- keep confidential information confidential
- offer suggestions rather than criticize others in the group
- be open with their thoughts
- participate in the group
- ask questions as appropriate to clarify or enhance ideas
- start on time and end on time
- expect to receive minutes or notes from the meeting within 24 hours of the meeting
- turn cell phones to vibrate and turn off blackberries or computers
- express thanks to those who do something special
- take a "pulse check" at the end of the meeting to ensure that everyone feels that he or she is being heard.

During this meeting, participants should not

- place blame or "finger point"
- interrupt others
- make fun or ridicule other peoples' ideas
- monopolize the conversation.

- ask the group if they want minutes, and ask for a volunteer to be note taker (be sensitive that some women are offended if they are asked to be the secretary)
- make sure participants know at the end of the meeting what to do and what their responsibilities are.

Learners' Roles in Facilitated Learning and Meeting Special Challenges

Participants should enter a facilitated learning experience with the expectation that they will get out of it what they put into it. They should not expect the facilitator to tell them the answer (like instructors do). Nor should they hold back, waiting to hear what higher-status individuals want to do.

Cultural differences will affect the level of participation in facilitated groups. For example, in some Asian cultures, there may be reluctance for lower-status individuals to participate. This is a challenge for facilitators, and there are many ways to handle it. One way is to have everyone write down what he or she thinks. Another issue is that, in some cultures, there is more than one meaning for *yes*. Facilitators should push to clarify what yes means and even ask group members what they will *do*. Cultural informants can be helpful to facilitators by monitoring what people say and how they say it. During breaks, facilitators may pointedly ask the cultural informants what is happening in the group and what it really means.

As noted in previous chapters, adult educators and trainers who serve as facilitators may face unique challenges when then deal with today's learners. Free agent learners are impatient and expect to have answers to their questions quickly and in a useful format, such as tools or in other practical ways. Most of today's learners are under pressure, since their work may be building up while they are participating in facilitated events. They may want to move faster than their progress deserves. Some learners resist the call for involvement and participation, and facilitators may need to find out what is behind that reluctance. Do they fear for their jobs? Are they worried that if they share their true feelings they may get into trouble somehow?

Of course, one way to overcome these problems is to move beyond facilitated learning events to action learning events in which participants are given a problem, objective, or goal, or an issue to address. The facilitator's role is to help ensure the effective interaction of group members so that they learn from one another as they attack a real-world problem. The group may elect (or management may appoint) a team leader whose role is to lead the group through task accomplishment. Action learning teams may work together face-to-face, by computer, or through a combination of online and on-site work. Action learning, particularly online, is also a way to give workers exposure to the thinking of other functional areas of the business or other national cultures represented in the company. If time does not permit job rotation, action learning can be a powerful alternative strategy.

Facilitator Competencies and Behaviors

A *competency* is, of course, a characteristic of an ideal performer. Competencies may be measured by *behavioral indicators*, which reveal behaviors associated with the demonstration of the competency. Competencies may also be measured by *work outputs*, the outcomes associated with the demonstration of a competency, and *quality indicators*, which clarify how the quality of a work output is determined.

Several competency studies have been undertaken to determine what kind of person a facilitator should ideally be. ASTD's own competency study *Mapping the Future* (Bernthal et al., 2004) lists "facilitating organizational change" as one area of expertise (AOE) associated with success in workplace learning and performance.

Many facilitator competency studies can be accessed simply by going to any Internet search engine and typing in "facilitator competencies." One website offers competency studies or lists of facilitator competencies compiled from numerous writers and authors (http://www.albany.edu/cpr/gf/resources/Facilitator Competencies.html). Other websites list the copyrighted facilitation competencies prepared by various organizations (for instance, http://www.symfonys.com/fac_comp.htm and http://www.nfdb.com/nfdb/competencies.htm).

One even focuses on competencies unique to online facilitators (http://www.ncsl.org.uk/mediastore/image2/facilitatorstoolkit/competencies.html). But one well-known competency study, also the basis for a professional certification in facilitation, is that of the International Association of Facilitators (http://www.iaf-world.org/i4a/pages/Index.cfm?pageid=3331). These competencies are listed in Exhibit 8-2. Review them, and compare your own level of competencies to them. Ask others for their impressions of your level of need for professional development on these competencies.

Exhibit 8-2: International Association of Facilitators' Core Competencies for Certification

Initial work on the competencies for facilitators began in 1991. IAF published **"Facilitator Competencies"** in *Group Facilitation: A Research and Applications Journal* in Winter 2000—Volume #2, Number 2. Also published at that time were several commentaries by IAF members with suggestions for further refinement. This revision, for the purpose of certification, was completed in February 2003.

IAF's work has identified the following six areas of core competency:

A. Create Collaborative Client Relationships	**B.** Plan Appropriate Group Processes	**C.** Create and Sustain a Participatory Environment	**D.** Guide Group to Appropriate and Useful Outcomes	**E.** Build and Maintain Professional Knowledge	**F.** Model Positive Professional Attitude

A. Create Collaborative Client Relationships

1. **Develop working partnerships**
   - Clarify mutual commitment
   - Develop consensus on tasks, deliverables, roles, and responsibilities
   - Demonstrate collaborative values and processes such as in cofacilitation
2. **Design and customize applications to meet client needs**
   - Analyze organizational environment
   - Diagnose client need
   - Create appropriate designs to achieve intended outcomes
   - Predefine a quality product and outcomes with client
3. **Manage multisession events effectively**
   - Contract with client for scope and deliverables
   - Develop event plan
   - Deliver event successfully
   - Assess/evaluate client satisfaction at all stages of the event or project

B. Plan Appropriate Group Processes

1. **Select clear methods and processes that**
   - Foster open participation with respect for client culture, norms, and participant diversity
   - Engage the participation of those with varied learning/thinking styles
   - Achieve a high quality product/outcome that meets the client needs
2. **Prepare time and space to support group process**
   - Arrange physical space to support the purpose of the meeting
   - Plan effective use of time
   - Provide effective atmosphere and drama for sessions

C. Create and Sustain a Participatory Environment

1. **Demonstrate effective participatory and interpersonal communication skills**
   - Apply a variety of participatory processes
   - Demonstrate effective verbal communication skills
   - Develop rapport with participants
   - Practice active listening
   - Demonstrate ability to observe and provide feedback to participants

(continued on next page)

Exhibit 8-2: International Association of Facilitators' Core Competencies for Certification (continued)

C. Create and Sustain a Participatory Environment (continued)

2. Honor and recognize diversity, ensuring inclusiveness
- Encourage positive regard for the experience and perception of all participants
- Create a climate of safety and trust
- Create opportunities for participants to benefit from the diversity of the group
- Cultivate cultural awareness and sensitivity

3. Manage group conflict
- Help individuals identify and review underlying assumptions
- Recognize conflict and its role within group learning/maturity
- Provide a safe environment for conflict to surface
- Manage disruptive group behavior
- Support the group through resolution of conflict

4. Evoke group creativity
- Draw out participants of all learning and thinking styles
- Encourage creative thinking
- Accept all ideas
- Use approaches that best fit needs and abilities of the group
- Stimulate and tap group energy

D. Guide Group to Appropriate and Useful Outcomes

1. Guide the group with clear methods and processes
- Establish clear context for the session
- Actively listen, question, and summarize to elicit the sense of the group
- Recognize tangents and redirect to the task
- Manage small and large group process

2. Facilitate group self-awareness about its task
- Vary the pace of activities according to needs of the group
- Identify information the group needs, and draw out data and insight from the group
- Help the group synthesize patterns, trends, root causes, frameworks for action
- Assist the group in reflection on its experience

3. Guide the group to consensus and desired outcomes
- Use a variety of approaches to achieve group consensus
- Use a variety of approaches to meet group objectives
- Adapt processes to changing situations and needs of the group
- Assess and communicate group progress
- Foster task completion

E. Build and Maintain Professional Knowledge

1. Maintain a base of knowledge
- Knowledgeable in management, organizational systems and development, group development, psychology, and conflict resolution
- Understand dynamics of change
- Understand learning and thinking theory

2. Know a range of facilitation methods
- Understand problem solving and decision-making models
- Understand a variety of group methods and techniques
- Know consequences of misuse of group methods
- Distinguish process from task and content
- Learn new processes, methods, and models in support of client's changing/emerging needs

E. Build and Maintain Professional Knowledge (continued)

3. Maintain professional standing

- Engage in ongoing study/learning related to our field
- Continuously gain awareness of new information in our profession
- Practice reflection and learning
- Build personal industry knowledge and networks
- Maintain certification

F. Model Positive Professional Attitude

1. Practice self-assessment and self-awareness

- Reflect on behavior and results
- Maintain congruence between actions and personal and professional values
- Modify personal behavior/style to reflect the needs of the group
- Cultivate understanding of one's own values and their potential impact on work with clients

2. Act with integrity

- Demonstrate a belief in the group and its possibilities
- Approach situations with authenticity and a positive attitude
- Describe situations as facilitator sees them, and inquire into different views
- Model professional boundaries and ethics (as described in ethics and values statement)

3. Trust group potential and model neutrality

- Honor the wisdom of the group
- Encourage trust in the capacity and experience of others
- Be vigilant to minimize influence on group outcomes
- Maintain an objective, nondefensive, nonjudgmental stance

Source: http://www.iaf-world.org/i4a/pages/Index.cfm?pageid=3331. Used by permission of IAF.

Most competency studies for facilitators center on the steps of a group process. Here is what facilitators in face-to-face situations must usually do:

Prepare for the facilitated session

- Establish an agenda
- Prepare questions
- Gather background information about the issues facing the group and the people in the group.

Open the facilitated session

- Manage introductions
- Clarify ground rules
- Review agenda with the group
- Ask for a volunteer to take notes/minutes, and distribute them later.

Manage the group interaction during the facilitated session

- Pose questions frequently
- Note responses on flipchart

- Watch group dynamics, ensuring that everyone is involved and participates
- Monitor the agenda to ensure effective use of time
- Call participants to account if ground rules are violated
- Surface issues/problems from the group
- Secure agreement from the group about the relative importance of the issues or problems they identified
- Identify possible solutions to the problems from the group using methods such as multivoting
- Secure agreement from the group on a solution (or solutions)
- Demonstrate appropriate use of small group methods (such as nominal group technique, Delphi technique, brainstorming, and others)
- Identify possible action plans to implement solutions from the group
- Secure agreement from the group on action plans
- Identify metrics and evaluation methods by which to measure success in implementing the solution
- Secure agreement from the group on the metrics and evaluation methods.

Conclude the facilitated session

- Ask group members if the important questions were addressed
- Clarify who has accepted assignments to be completed after the session
- Check that the minutes will be distributed on a timely basis
- Ask participants if there are other issues to address in future meetings
- Process group interaction by inviting group members to discuss ways that they could improve interpersonal interaction
- Encourage continued actions by the group, perhaps by establishing an online site for group members to continue their interaction virtually.

Rate yourself on these facilitation competencies in Exhibit 8-3.

Differences Among On-Site, Online, and Blended Format Facilitator Behaviors

Some people believe that significant differences exist between the facilitation skills required for face-to-face interaction in small groups and facilitation skills online or using other forms of technology (such as webcams or teleconferences). But the reality is that the competencies essential for a good facilitator are pretty much the same regardless of venue. It is true, however, that online and other electronically

Exhibit 8-3: Getting It Done Assessment for Facilitation

Directions: Use this assessment form to rate yourself on professional development needs with regards to various facilitator competencies and the behaviors associated with them. For each competency and behavior listed in the left column below, rate yourself according to need for professional development in the right column by circling a number using the following scale:

1 = No need for professional development
2 = Some need for professional development
3 = A need for professional development
4 = A great need for professional development

When you finish, discuss your identified needs with your supervisor or with appropriately skilled professional mentors who may give you advice about how to meet your professional development needs.

Competency/Behavior	Need for Professional Development			
	No need	**Some need**	**Need**	**Great need**
Prepare for the facilitated session	**1**	**2**	**3**	**4**
Establish an agenda	1	2	3	4
Prepare questions	1	2	3	4
Gather background information about the issues facing the group and the people in the group	1	2	3	4
Open the facilitated session	**1**	**2**	**3**	**4**
Manage introductions	1	2	3	4
Clarify ground rules	1	2	3	4
Review agenda with the group	1	2	3	4
Ask for a volunteer to take notes/ minutes, and distribute them later	1	2	3	4
Manage the group interaction during the facilitated session	**1**	**2**	**3**	**4**
Pose questions frequently	1	2	3	4
Note responses on flipchart	1	2	3	4
Watch group dynamics, ensuring that everyone is involved and participates	1	2	3	4
Monitor the agenda to ensure effective use of time	1	2	3	4
Call participants to account if ground rules are violated	1	2	3	4
Surface issues/problems from the group	1	2	3	4
Secure agreement from the group about the relative importance of the issues or problems they identified	1	2	3	4

(continued on next page)

Exhibit 8-3: Getting It Done Assessment for Facilitation (continued)

Competency/Behavior	Need for Professional Development			
	No need	**Some need**	**Need**	**Great need**
Identify possible solutions to the problems from the group using methods such as multivoting	1	2	3	4
Secure agreement from the group on a solution (or solutions)	1	2	3	4
Demonstrate appropriate use of small group methods (such as nominal group technique, Delphi technique, brainstorming, and others)	1	2	3	4
Identify possible action plans to implement solutions from the group	1	2	3	4
Secure agreement from the group on action plans	1	2	3	4
Identify metrics and evaluation methods by which to measure success in implementing the solution	1	2	3	4
Secure agreement from the group on the metrics and evaluation methods	1	2	3	4
Conclude the facilitated session	**1**	**2**	**3**	**4**
Ask group members if the important questions were addressed	1	2	3	4
Clarify who has accepted assignments to be completed after the session	1	2	3	4
Check that the minutes will be distributed on a timely basis	1	2	3	4
Ask participants if there are other issues to address in future meetings	1	2	3	4
Process group interaction by inviting group members to discuss ways that they could improve interpersonal interaction	1	2	3	4
Encourage continued actions by the group, perhaps by establishing an online site for group members to continue their interaction virtually	1	2	3	4

mediated facilitation may require special competencies in using the technology. A major goal in using technology assistance is to prevent it from getting in the way or becoming a barrier to group interaction.

Basic Rule 7

The competencies essential for a good facilitator are pretty much the same regardless of venue.

Consider the use of online learning. For online learning to be effective, facilitators must make it easy for the learner to use the technology. This often means that the learning experience should open with a welcome page that stipulates the technology required to access the learning experience. Many problems in online facilitated events can be prevented if learners know what browser they are using, what version of it they are using, and what level of RAM their computer runs with. Surprisingly, many people do not know—even today. If possible, the technology itself should run a diagnostic to prompt the learner about what requirements may be lacking.

Here are a few special tips for facilitators who work with online instruction:

Opening the Facilitated Online Session

- Clarify the technology requirements, and invite participants to check that they have the necessary technology to participate effectively.
- Collect personal information from participants—whatever they feel comfortable sharing—but make clear what is absolutely essential (such as email addresses).
- Find a way to have students introduce themselves, perhaps by posting an introduction online or (if they feel comfortable doing it) posting a picture. (Some facilitators even go so far as to solicit the MyFace or YouTube information from students and encourage them to cross-post to their listings on these social networking sites.)
- Clarify how the learning experience will be conducted and what is expected of participants. (Note assignments, if any, and deadlines—especially ones established right at the outset of the course—so that learners know what to do immediately.)

Facilitating the Course

- Note expectations about how participants are expected to participate, such as by answering posted questions from the facilitator.
- Note special expectations, such as office hours when participants may call the facilitator, the use of special chat rooms for group interaction and how they are assigned, times when the facilitator will be online with a webcast, times when participants are expected to be available for teleconferences, or times when instant messaging may be used.
- Give participants an early assignment so that they are required to use the technology and become more comfortable with it.
- Post special questions for participants periodically.
- Provide resources to participants to access, such as readings, web links, or even videos posted online.
- Find ways to get participants to work together to achieve common learning goals, such as case study analysis.
- Provide evaluation cues so that participants can self-assess themselves and are clear about expectations.

Concluding the Workshop

- Poll participants about what they have learned and how well they learned it.
- Ask participants for ways to improve interaction and group process in subsequent sessions.

Improving Facilitation Skills

Facilitation is action oriented. The best way to improve facilitation skills is to practice them, receive feedback on performance from participants and from more skilled professional mentors, and then use that feedback to improve subsequent facilitation experiences. Some ambitious facilitators may also choose to videotape their own facilitated sessions and view them later to identify their own areas for improvement. Of course, some facilitators may choose to pursue professional certification, which will require them to demonstrate facilitation skills and receive feedback on it.

Still another approach to hone facilitation skills is to apply social learning theory. Take steps to participate in sessions facilitated by masters. Watch carefully how they facilitate, take notes on what they do, and then seek to imitate those behaviors in one's own facilitation experiences. Working directly under the tutelage of a skilled facilitator can also be a powerful way to build skills and receive excellent feedback for future skill building.

The future for adult learning facilitation in all media is bright. There will be increasing demand for facilitators of all kinds.

Getting It Done

In chapter 8, you learned what a *facilitator* is, how a facilitator is different from an *instructor*, what facilitators should do to clarify roles and set ground rules with groups, what learners should do in facilitated learning, and how the unique characteristics of today's adult learners pose special challenges to facilitators. You also learned what competencies and behaviors are associated with facilitation, how facilitator behaviors differ, depending on whether learning is delivered on site, online, or in a blended format, and what can be done to improve facilitation skills.

1. Summarize the competencies essential to a facilitator.

   ____

   ____

   ____

2. What differences might exist between what a facilitator should do in face-to-face interactions and in technology-mediated instruction, such as online or web-based learning experiences? List and explain what the differences are and why they are important.

   ____

   ____

   ____

3. List each competency of a facilitator and describe what you could do to build your competence as a facilitator.

   ____

   ____

   ____

9

Reading the Future of Adult Learning: Seven Hopeful Predictions

What's Inside This Chapter

In this chapter, you'll learn:

- Trends that could affect the future of adult learning
- The likely impact of those trends.

Numerous studies have been done about the future. It seems that every day someone comes out with the latest crystal ball reading. Consider reviewing ASTD's annual *State of the Industry Report*, the *State of the Industry* published each year by *Training Magazine*, and the general predictions for the future found on websites of organizations like the World Future Society (http://www.wfs.org/).

This chapter will focus on seven predictions for the future of adult learning:

1. There will be more focus on informal and incidental learning as means of building competencies.
2. There will be more appreciation for feelings, values, ethics, and cultural awareness among future learners and among future learning professionals.

3. There will be increasing interest in the special needs of older adult learners—those beyond traditional retirement age, who may remain in the workforce in the United States and in other nations.
4. There will be more sensitivity to diversity among trainers and adult educators, and diversity will be more broadly defined than race or gender.
5. Technology will continue unabated in its impact on learning experiences, and more emerging technologies will surface in the future that will affect the means by which people learn and the means by which learning professionals will reach their learners.
6. More attention will focus on building learner competencies in learning how to learn.
7. More attention will focus on the context in which learning occurs and how context affects learning.

Prediction 1: More Focus on Informal and Incidental Learning

Organizational decision makers and workers alike are becoming more familiar with alternatives to traditional, classroom-based, and even online or electronically mediated instruction. Most people are beginning to realize that most development occurs on the job and in real time, not in classrooms and off the job.

Informal learning occurs through experience. It can occur at work, at home, and in other settings. People simply learn through all of their experiences. Informal learning occurs outside educational institutions, is not guided by a plan for instruction or learning, and is seamlessly woven into the experience of living.

Incidental learning is a consequence or byproduct of experience. By setting out to do one thing, individuals learn other things along the way through hands-on experience, observation, and talking or interacting with others. Even failures and mistakes provide lessons of incidental learning.

While neither informal nor incidental learning lend themselves to being easily planned or managed—after all, their unplanned nature is what makes them what they are—they are nevertheless attracting attention as a repository of what many people have actually learned in their lives. They can be enhanced. They can be catalogued. They can be cross-matched with experience and with competencies.

Prediction 2: More Appreciation for Feelings, Values, Ethics, and Cultural Awareness

There is more to learning—and more to work performance—than simply "knowing" (cognition). Traditional schooling, however, has emphasized knowledge acquisition and retention. And yet the human experience of learning is more complex. Its full complexity should be appreciated, and other elements of that experience beyond knowledge should be considered.

For this reason, the future will hold growing interest in feelings, values, ethics, and cultural awareness. For some people, that is not comfortable territory. Should adult educators and trainers get into feelings? How much should organizations police values? What about ethical considerations—and how can they be made clear amid many shades of gray? How can cultural awareness be taught and learned? These and other questions will garner increasing interest as emotional intelligence gains acceptance, organizational leaders struggle with handling scandals stemming from values and ethical issues, and globalization brings cultural awareness increasingly to the fore.

Prediction 3: Increasing Interest in the Special Needs of Older Adult Learners

In 2006, the oldest Baby Boomers turned 60 years old. At this writing, a Boomer turns 50 every seven seconds. The future impact of Boomers on adult learning should not be minimized. When Boomers progressed through schools, they transformed them, prompting new building—and new techniques. When Boomers entered higher education, they prompted nations to build up their universities. As Boomers entered the workforce, they transformed it. And now, as Boomers prepare for retirement, they are likely to revolutionize thinking about what retirement means. Many Boomers will not be able to afford traditional retirement—sailing off into the sunset for the rest of their lives. They may not have the pensions (or social security) to afford it, and they may not be able to afford the double-digit health care increases that have characterized the U.S. economy in recent years. Consequently, many Boomers may end up delaying retirement, and others may choose to work simply to stay active and involved in life.

But one thing is clear: When roughly 78 million people of the U.S. workforce are at or beyond retirement age, both government and employers will pay attention to the special needs of older people.

Right now, stereotypes about the elderly do not match up to what research shows. The stereotype is that "you can't teach an old dog new tricks." But research indicates that older workers, though participating less often in traditional education than members of many other age categories, possess no real difference in learning ability. While it has been shown that they may take longer to learn new things than younger people, this may not reflect inability so much as extra caution. Additionally, older people do face the diminution of their senses—touch, taste, smell, sight, and hearing.

More attention in the future will undoubtedly focus on learning among older adult workers. Is there anything special about them? If so, what is it?

Prediction 4: Increasing Sensitivity to Diversity Among Trainers and Adult Educators

Diversity means more than differences of race or gender. Generation Y is the most diverse generation, and the sheer numbers in that group will gradually build awareness of the full range of diversity. One way to think about it is that diversity means accepting, celebrating, and appreciating people regardless of age, race, gender, socioeconomic status, ethnic background, physical or mental ability, sexual orientation, religion, language, citizenship status, or veteran status. Diversity includes also appreciation for other value systems as well, permitting people to dissent from what they truly do not believe in.

Adult educators and trainers will face growing interest in showing appreciation for a broad mix of people from varied backgrounds and across many cultures. With the growing use of online instruction, people will also increasingly communicate globally. This will prompt growing interest in how national cultural affects participation in online or other electronically mediated instruction.

Prediction 5: Technology's Impact on Learning Will Continue Unabated

Adult educators and trainers associated with the business community continue to be enamored with instructional technology and its impact on learning. While approaches to teaching have remained largely unchanged in many educational institutions, technology has advanced rapidly. In 1970, few people could conceive of technology as it exists today. If present trends in the growth of computing power and cost continue, it is conceivable that artificially intelligent robots will be on the market—and have the thinking power to rival a human being—by 2020. Groups like the World Future Society have even predicted that human beings may have chips surgically implanted in their heads—giving them wireless Internet access at all times—within a decade. While these predictions seem hard to believe, consider that common use of the personal computer has only been around since the mid-1980s. That is a short time indeed in the scheme of things. It is likely that, in the future, adult educators will increasingly find that they can offer learning experiences across a broad range of channels, using new and emerging media, and that many learners will find such high-tech approaches appealing.

Prediction 6: More Attention Will Focus on Building Learner Competencies in Learning How to Learn

As noted in earlier chapters, the decided trend in the field of adult learning is to reduce the teacher or trainer's burden in training and dramatically increase the learner's burden to assume initiative in the learning process. This trend will continue—and will intensify. One reason for that is that technology-assisted learning places more responsibility on the learner. Another reason is that it is consistent with the personal improvement philosophy that has emerged in recent years. Individuals are taking more responsibility for their nutrition, their exercise, their "carbon footprints," and their careers. It just makes sense that they would also be expected to take more responsibility for how they learn and for improving how they learn.

The problem is that individuals are still not given effective instruction on how to learn. Most people learn how to study and how to learn as part of an incidental learning process—that is, as a byproduct of their other learning experiences. Few have had instruction on how to improve their study skills and how to take initiative for their own learning projects.

Prediction 7: More Attention Will Focus on the Context in Which Learning Occurs

As business continues to go global, more attention will be paid to how national culture, organizational culture, and even team work affects learning. How are individuals influenced by the context in which they live and work? As business leaders

Exhibit 9-1: A Worksheet to Address the Future of Adult Learning

Directions: Use this worksheet to organize your thinking on seven predictions about the future of adult learning and how you and your organization can prepare for them. For each prediction in the left column below, indicate in the center column what that might mean for you and your organization, and indicate in the right column what you and your organization should do now to prepare for these future challenges.

	Predictions	What Might the Prediction Mean to You and Your Organization?	What Should You and Your Organization Do to Prepare for These Future Challenges?
1	There will be more focus on informal and incidental learning as means of building competencies.		
2	There will be more appreciation for feelings, values, ethics, and cultural awareness among future learners and among future learning professionals.		
3	There will be increasing interest in the special needs of older adult learners—those beyond traditional retirement age, who may remain in the workforce in the United States and in other nations.		
4	There will be more sensitivity to diversity among trainers and adult educators, and diversity will be more broadly defined than race or gender.		
5	Technology will continue unabated in its impact on learning experiences, and more emerging technologies will surface in the future that will affect the means by which people learn and the means by which learning professionals will reach their learners.		
6	More attention will focus on building learner competencies in learning how to learn.		
7	More attention will focus on the context in which learning occurs and how context affects learning.		

pursue the promise of the learning organization and seek to build cultures that encourage organizational learning, the role of context will only grow in importance. A future goal will be to establish corporate cultures in which people feel encouraged to learn on their own to solve work-related problems in real time.

What Should Learning Professionals Do?

The future of adult learning seems bright. Learning is the means by which talent is unleashed. Most business leaders concede that the key to future competitive success will be the ability to leverage talent and innovation.

Getting It Done

In chapter 9, you learned about trends that could affect the future of adult learning and what might be the likely impact of those trends. Complete the activity appearing in Exhibit 9-1 to indicate what you think the seven trends described in this chapter will mean and how they might affect you and your organization.

References

Abdullah, M.H. (2001). *Self-directed Learning* [ERIC digest No. 169]. Bloomington, IN: ERIC Clearinghouse on Reading, English, and Communication. (ERIC Document Reproduction Service No. ED459458).

Anderson, L. & Krathwohl, D. (2001). *A Taxonomy for Learning, Teaching and Assessing: A Revision of Bloom's Taxonomy of Educational Objectives.* New York: Longman.

Argyris, C. & Schön, D. (1978). *Organizational Learning: A Theory of Action Perspective.* Reading, MA: Addison-Wesley.

Ausubel, D. (1963). *The Psychology of Meaningful Verbal Learning.* New York: Grune & Stratton.

Barber, C.E. (2005). *Age-Related Changes in Memory.* No. 10.243. http://www.ext.colostate .edu/Pubs/consumer/10243.html.

Beck, K. (1997). *Organizational Learning.* http://www.sfb504.uni-mannheim.de/ glossary/orglearn.htm.

Bernthal, P., Colteryahn, K., Davis, P., Naughton, J., Rothwell, W., & Wellins, R. (2004). *Mapping the Future: Shaping New Workplace Learning and Performance Competencies.* Alexandria, VA: ASTD Press.

Bloom, B., & Krathwohl, D. (1956). *Taxonomy of Educational Objectives: The Classification of Educational Goals. Handbook I: Cognitive Domain.* New York: Longman, Green.

Bransford, J.D., et al. (1990). Anchored Instruction: Why We Need It and How Technology Can Help. In *Cognition, Education and Multimedia,* D. Nix & R. Sprio (Eds.). Hillsdale, NJ: Erlbaum Associates.

Carnevale A., Gainer, L., & Meltzer, A. (1990). *Workplace Basics: The Essential Skills Employers Want.* San Francisco: Jossey-Bass.

Carroll, J.M. (1998). *Minimalism Beyond the Nurnberg Funnel.* Cambridge, MA: MIT Press.

Chapter 4: Instructional Analysis: Analyzing the Learners. http://www.angelfire.com/la2/ learners/learners.html.

Cyert, R.M., & March, J.G. (1963). *A Behavioral Theory of the Firm.* Englewood Cliffs, NJ.

Dodgson, M. (1991). Technology, Learning, Technology Strategy and Competitive Pressures. *British Journal of Management*, 2/3, 132–149.

Douglass, W. (2001—updated 2007). http://www.ext.colostate.edu/pubs/octnews/oc01101.htm.

Earley, C.P., & Mosakowski, E. (2004). Cultural Intelligence. *Harvard Business Review, 82* (10): 139–146.

Endorf, M., & McNeff, M. (1991). The Adult Learner: Five Types. *Adult Learning, 2* (7), 20–25.

Erikson, E. (1994). *Identity and the Life Cycle.* New York: W.W. Norton & Company.

Finger, M., & Brand, S.B. (1999). The Concept of the "Learning Organization" Applied to the Transformation of the Public Sector. In *Organizational Learning and the Learning Organization*, M. Easterby-Smith, L. Araujo, & J. Burgoyne (Eds.). London: Sage.

Fiol, C., & Lyles, M. (1985). Organizational Learning. *Academy of Management Review, 10*(4):803–813.

Gagnè, R. (1985). *The Conditions of Learning.* 4th ed. New York: Holt, Rinehart & Winston.

Gardner, H. (1983). *Frames of Mind.* New York: Basic Books.

Geiger, H. (2007). *Myths of E-Learning Interactivity.* http://www.ptrain.com/articles/myths.htm.

Gillett, A. (1997). *Intercultural Communication.* http://www.uefap.com/articles/arena.htm.

Goleman, D. (1997). *Emotional Intelligence: Why It Can Matter More Than IQ.* New York: Bantam.

Gronlund, N.E. (1970). *Stating Behavioral Objectives for Classroom Instruction.* New York: Macmillan.

Gross, R. *Your Learning and Your Brain: Five Ways to Enhance Your Learning.* http://adulted.about.com/od/learningstyles/a/brain.htm.

Grow, G. (1991—updated 1996). *Teaching Learners to be Self-Directed.* http://longleaf.net/ggrow.

Guild, P., & Garger, S. (1998). *Marching to Different Drummers.* 2nd ed. Washington, DC: American Society for Curriculum Development.

Hampden-Turner, C., & Trompenaars, F. (1997). *Riding the Waves of Culture: Understanding Diversity in Global Business.* 2nd ed. New York: McGraw-Hill.

Harrow, A. (1972). *A Taxonomy of the Psychomotor Domain. A Guide for Developing Behavioral Objectives.* New York: McKay.

Havighurst, R. (1972). *Developmental Tasks and Education.* 3rd ed. London: Longman Group.

Hergenhahn, B., & Olson, M. (1997). *Introduction to the Theories of Learning.* 5th ed. Upper Saddle Creek, NJ: Prentice-Hall.

Hofstede, G. (1986). Cultural Differences in Teaching and Learning. *International Journal of Intercultural Relations, 10*(3), 301–320.

Hofstede, G. (1991). *Culture and Organizations.* New York: Harper-Collins.

Howell, S., Williams, P., & Lindsay, N. (2003). Thirty-Two Trends Affecting Distance Education: An Informed Foundation for Strategic Planning. *Online Journal of Distance Learning Administration, 6*(3). http://www.westga.edu/~distance/ojdla/fall63/howell63.html.

Kelly, H. Interactivity in Online Courses. http://www.studyoverseas.com/distance/interactivity.htm.

Knowles, M. (1975). *Self-Directed Learning.* Chicago: Follet.

Knowles, M. (1984). *The Adult Learner: A Neglected Species.* 3rd ed. Houston, TX: Gulf Publishing.

Knowles, M. (1984). *Andragogy in Action.* San Francisco: Jossey-Bass.

Kolb, D.A. (1984). *Experiential Learning.* Englewood Cliffs, NJ: Prentice-Hall.

Krathwohl, D., Bloom, B., & Masia, B. (1964). *Taxonomy of Educational Objectives: The Classification of Educational Goals. Handbook II: Affective Domain.* New York: David McKay Co.

Levinthal, D., & March, J. (1993). The Myopia of Learning. *Strategic Management Journal,* 14, 95–112.

Levinson, D.J., with Darrow, C.N., & Klein, E.B. (1978). *Seasons of a Man's Life.* New York: Random House.

Levitt, B., & March J. (1988). Organizational Learning. *Annual Review of Sociology,* 14:319–340.

Long, H.B. *Skills for Self-Directed Learning.* http://faculty-staff.ou.edu/L/Huey.B.Long-1/Articles/sd/selfdirected.html.

McLellan, H. (1995). *Situated Learning Perspectives.* Englewood Cliffs, NJ: Educational Technology Publications.

March, J., & Olsen, J. (1975). The Uncertainty of the Past: Organizational Learning under Ambiguity. *European Journal of Political Research,* 3, 147–171.

Moravec, H. (1997). *When Will Computer Hardware Match the Human Brain?* http://www.transhumanist.com/volume1/moravec.htm.

Norman, D. (1967). *Memory and Attention.* New York: Wiley.

Pask, G. (1975). *Conversation, Cognition, and Learning.* New York: Elsevier.

Rados, C. (May–June 2005). Sound Advice About Age-Related Hearing Loss. *FDA Consumer magazine.* http://www.fda.gov/fdac/features/2005/305_hear.html.

Rogers, C. (1969). *Freedom to Learn.* Columbus, OH: Merrill.

Rogers, C.R., & Freiberg, H.J. (1994). *Freedom to Learn.* 3rd ed. Columbus, OH: Merrill/Macmillan.

Rosenzweig, M., & Bennett, E. (1996). Psychobiology of Plasticity: Effects of Training and Experience on Brain and Behavior. *Behavioural Brain Research*, 78: 57–65.

Rothwell, W. (1999). *The Action Learning Guidebook*. San Francisco: Pfeiffer.

Rothwell, W.J. (2000). *Models for the Workplace Learner.* Unpublished research report.

Rothwell, W. (2002). *The Workplace Learner*. New York: AMACOM.

Rothwell, W., & Kazanas, H. (2008). *Mastering the Instructional Design Process: A Systematic Approach*. 4th ed. San Francisco: Jossey-Bass/Pfeiffer.

Rothwell, W., Butler, M., Maldonado, C., Hunt, D., Peters, K., Li, J., & Stern, J. (2006). *Handbook of Training Technology: An Introductory Guide to Facilitating Learning With Technology—From Planning Through Evaluation*. San Francisco: Pfeiffer.

Rothwell, W., Sterns, H., Spokus, D., and Reaser, J. (2008). *Working Longer: New Strategies for Managing, Training, and Retaining Older Employees*. New York: AMACOM.

Schein, E. (1992). *Organizational Culture and Leadership*. San Francisco: Jossey-Bass.

Selkoe, D. (1996 September). Aging Brain, Aging Mind. *Scientific American,* 135–142.

Senge, P. (1990). *The Fifth Discipline: The Art and Practice of the Learning Organization*. New York: Currency Doubleday.

Sheehey, G. (2006). *Passages: Predictable Crises of Adult Life*. New York: Ballantine.

Smith, M. (2001). *The Learning Organization*. http://www.infed.org/biblio/learning-organization.htm.

Sweller, J. (1999). *Instructional Design in Technical Areas*. Camberwell, Victoria, Australia: Australian Council for Educational Research.

Tough, A. (1971). *The Adult's Learning Projects: A Fresh Approach to Theory and Practice in Adult Learning*. Toronto: OISE Press.

Vision Loss from Eye Disorders Will Increase as Americans Age. (2004). http://www.nei.nih.gov/news/pressreleases/041204.asp.

Wenger, E. (1998). *Communities of Practice: Learning, Meaning, and Identity*. New York: Cambridge University Press.

Wikipedia. "Learning." http://en.wikipedia.org/wiki/Learning.

Additional Resources

Barer-Stein, T., & Kompf, M. (2001). *The Craft of Teaching Adults.* Toronto: Irwin Publishing.

Biech, E. (2005). *Training for Dummies.* Indianapolis, IN: Wiley.

Brockett, R., & Hiemstra, R. (1991). *Self-Direction in Adult Learning: Perspectives on Theory, Research, and Practice.* http://home.twcny.rr.com/hiemstra/sdlindex.html.

Brookfield, S. (1988). Developing Critically Reflective Practitioners: A Rationale for Training Educators of Adults. In *Training Educators of Adults: The Theory and Practice of Graduate Adult Education*. New York: Routledge.

Brookfield, S. (1989). *Developing Critical Thinkers: Challenging Adults to Explore Alternative Ways of Thinking and Acting.* San Francisco: Jossey-Bass.

Brookfield, S. (1995). Adult Learning: An Overview. In *International Encyclopedia of Education*, A. Tuinjman (Ed.). Oxford: Pergamon Press.

Brookfield, S. (1995). *Becoming a Critically Reflective Teacher.* San Francisco: Jossey-Bass.

Brown, J., Collins, A., & Duguid, P. (1993). *Situated Cognition and the Culture of Learning.* http://www.ilt.columbia.edu/ilt/papers/JohnBrown.html.

Brundage, D., & MacKeracher, D. (1980). *Adult Learning Principles and Their Application to Program Planning.* Toronto: Ontario Institute for Studies in Education.

Cromley, J. (2000). *Learning to Think: Learning to Learn.* National Institute for Literacy, U.S. Department of Education. http://www.ed.gov/about/ordering.jsp.

Cross, P. (1981). *Adults as Learners.* San Francisco: Jossey-Bass.

Cross, P. (1992). *Adults as Learners: Increasing Participation and Facilitating Learning.* Toronto: Wiley & Sons.

Dirkx, J., & Prenger, S. (1997). *A Guide for Planning and Implementing Instruction for Adults: A Theme-Based Approach.* San Francisco: Jossey-Bass.

Gardner, H. (1993a). *Frames of Mind: The Theory of Multiple Intelligences, 10th Anniversary Edition.* New York: Basic Books.

Gardner, H. (1993b). *Multiple Intelligences: The Theory in Practice.* New York: Basic Books.

Gardner, H. (2003). *Multiple Intelligences After Twenty Years.* http://pzweb.harvard.edu/PIs/HG_MI_after_20_years.pdf.

Gibbs, G. (1988). *Learning by Doing.* http://www.chelt.ac.uk/gdn/gibbs/index.htm.

Grabove, V. (1997). The Many Facets of Transformative Learning Theory and Practice. In *New Directions for Adult and Continuing Education,* 74, 89–95.

Hiemstra, R. (1991). Aspects of Effective Learning Environments. In *New Directions for Adult and Continuing Education,* 50, 5–12.

Hiemstra, R., & Brockett, R. (1994). From Behaviourism to Humanism. In H. Long & Associates, *New Ideas About Self-Directed Learning.* Norman, OK: Oklahoma Research Center for Continuing Professional and Higher Education, University of Oklahoma.

Hoare, C. (Ed.). (2006). *Handbook of Adult Development and Learning.* New York: Oxford.

Imel, S. (1995). *Inclusive Adult Learning Environments.* ERIC Digest #162. Available at http://ericacve.org/docs/adt-lrng.htm.

Imel, S. (1994). *Guidelines for Working with Adult Learners.* Available at http://ericfacility.net/ericdigests/ed377313.html.

Imel, S. (2000). *Contextual Learning in Adult Education.* Practice Application Brief No. 12. Available at http://ericacve.org/docgen.asp?tbl=pab&ID=102.

Kerka, S. (2002). *Teaching Adults: Is It Different?* ERIC Myths and Realities No. 19. Available at http://ericacve.org/docgen.asp?tbl=mr&id=111.

Knowles, M. (1975) *Self-Directed Learning. A Guide for Learners and Teachers.* Englewood Cliffs, NJ: Prentice Hall/Cambridge.

Knowles, M. (1980). *The Modern Practice of Adult Education: From Pedagogy to Andragogy.* Englewood Cliffs, NJ: Prentice Hall Regents.

Knowles, M., & Associates. (1984). *Andragogy in Action. Applying Modern Principles of Adult Education.* San Francisco: Jossey-Bass.

Knowles, M. (1990). *The Adult Learner: A Neglected Species.* 4th ed. Houston, TX: Gulf Publishing.

Knowles, M., Holton, E., & Swanson, R. (2005). *The Adult Learner: The Definitive Classic in Adult Education and Human Resource Development.* 5th ed. Burlington, MA: Elsevier.

MacKeracher, D. (1996). *Making Sense of Adult Learning.* Toronto: Culture Concepts.

Marsick, V., & Watkins, K. (2001). Informal and Incidental Learning. In *The New Update on Adult Learning Theory,* S. Merriam (Ed.). San Francisco: Jossey-Bass.

Massari, J. *Age and Its Effects on Learning.* http://www.duke.edu/~kem2/cps1/Massari.htm.

Merriam, S. (2001). Andragogy and Self-Directed Learning: Pillars of Adult Learning Theory. In *The New Update on Adult Learning Theory,* S. Merriam (Ed.). San Francisco: Jossey-Bass.

Merriam, S., & Caffarella, R. (1999). *Learning in Adulthood.* San Francisco: Jossey-Bass.

Merriam, S., Caffarella, R., & Baumgartner, L. (2007). *Learning in Adulthood: A Comprehensive Guide.* San Francisco: Jossey-Bass.

McClusky, H. (1971). The Adult as Learner. In *Management of the Urban Crisis,* McNeil & Seashore (Eds.). New York: The Free Press.

Mezirow, J. (1997). Transformative Learning: Theory to Practice. *New Directions for Adult and Continuing Education,* 74, 5–11.

Mezirow, J. (1990). *Fostering Critical Reflection in Adulthood.* San Francisco: Jossey-Bass.

Mezirow, J. (1991). *Transformative Dimensions of Adult Learning.* San Francisco: Jossey-Bass.

Monts, R. (2000). *Andragogy or Pedagogy: A Discussion of Instructional Methodology for Adult Learners.* http://www.coe.ilstu.edu/scienceed/jinks/ci538/papers/monts.htm.

Perry, W. (1970). *Forms of Intellectual and Ethical Development in the College Years: A Scheme.* New York: Holt, Rinehart, and Winston.

Pratt, D.D. (Spring 1988). Andragogy as a Relational Construct. *Adult Education Quarterly 38*(3), 160–172.

Renner, P. (1999). *The Art of Teaching Adults.* Vancouver: Training Associates.

Rothwell, W. (1999). *The Action Learning Guidebook: A Real-Time Strategy for Problem-Solving, Training Design, and Employee Development.* San Francisco: Jossey-Bass/Pfeiffer.

Rothwell, W. (2002). *The Workplace Learner: How to Align Training Initiatives with Individual Learning Competencies.* New York: Amacom.

Rothwell, W., & Sensenig, K. (Eds.). (1999). *The Sourcebook for Self-Directed Learning.* Amherst, MA: Human Resource Development Press.

Schuman, S. (2005). *The IAF Handbook of Group Facilitation: Best Practices from the Leading Organization in Facilitation.* San Francisco: Jossey-Bass.

Stolovitch, H.D., & Keeps, E.J. (2002). *Telling Ain't Training.* Alexandria, VA: ASTD Press.

Taylor, M. (1986). Learning for Self-Direction in the Classroom: The Pattern of a Transition Process. *Studies in Higher Education, 11*(1), 55–72.

Taylor, K., Marienau, C., & Fiddler, M. (2000). *Developing Adult Learners: Strategies for Teachers and Trainers.* San Francisco: Jossey-Bass.

Vella, J., & Vella, J.K. (2000). *Taking Learning to Task: Creative Strategies for Teaching Adults.* Toronto: Wiley & Sons.

Vella, J., & Vella, J.K. (2002). *Learning to Listen, Learning to Teach: The Power of Dialogue in Educating Adults.* Toronto: Wiley & Sons.

Wlodkowski, R. (1999). *Enhancing Adult Motivation to Learn: A Comprehensive Guide to Teaching All Adults.* Rev. ed. San Francisco: Jossey-Bass.

Zinn, L.M. (1991). Identifying Your Philosophical Orientation. In *Adult Learning Methods,* M.W. Galbraith (Ed.). Malabar, FL: Krieger Publishing Company.

About the Author

William J. Rothwell, Ph.D., SPHR is professor of learning and performance in the Workforce Education and Development program, Department of Learning and Performance Systems, at the Pennsylvania State University, University Park campus. In that capacity, he heads up the number-two-ranked graduate program in learning and performance. He has written 64 books and authored, co-authored, edited, or co-edited 300 books, book chapters, and articles. Before arriving at Penn State in 1993, he had 20 years of work experience as a training director in government and in business. He has also worked as a consultant for more than 40 multinational corporations, including Motorola, General Motors, Ford, and many others. In 2004, he earned the Graduate Faculty Teaching Award at Pennsylvania State University, a single award given to the best graduate faculty member on the 23 campuses of the Penn State system. His train-the-trainer programs have won global awards for excellence from Motorola University and from Linkage Inc. His recent books include *HR Transformation* (Davies-Black, 2008) and *Working Longer* (Amacom, 2008). He was a major researcher for the last three international competency studies of ASTD, including *ASTD Models for Human Performance* (2nd ed., 2000), *ASTD Models for Workplace Learning and Performance* (1999), and *Mapping the Future* (2004). A frequent conference keynoter and seminar presenter both in the United States and in many other countries, he can be reached by email at wjr9@psu.edu.

Index

In this index, *e* stands for exhibit.